ITALY
from the air

Dedicated to Elisa and Toto

vmb
PUBLISHERS

ITALY
from the air

Photographs
Guido Alberto Rossi

Text
Carlo Grande

Graphic Design
Patrizia Balocco Lovisetti
Anna Galliani

Translation
Ann Ghiringhelli

Editors
Leslie Bockol
Irene Kleeberg

CONTENTS

VMB Publishers®
An imprint of White Star S.p.A., Italy
© 1997, 2007 White Star S.p.A.
Via Candido Sassone, 22/24
13100 Vercelli, Italy - www.whitestar.it

ISBN 13: 978-88-540-0830-4

Reprints:
1 2 3 4 5 6   11 10 09 08 07

Printed in China

1 Corniglia is one of the coastal villages that make up the famous Cinque Terre. It perches on terraced vineyards sloping down to the sea.

2-3 A region of boundless, awe-inspiring landscapes, Mont Blanc has fascinated visitors for centuries.

4-5 Isola Bella on Lake Maggiore, located between Stresa and Baveno, is the foremost of three Borromean islands. It has a splendid terraced garden with many rare and exotic plants. Visitors to this delightful spot enjoy fine views over the chilly waters of the lake.

6-7 The rocky island of Lampedusa was uninhabited until 1843, when Ferdinand of Bourbon encouraged the immigration of fisherman. The island covers eight square miles and is famous for the caretta-caretta turtles which lay their eggs along its shores.

8 The breathtaking Leaning Tower of Pisa is an extraordinary piece of architecture. Its elegant columns are made of precious marble.

9 Verona's Arena is the Roman amphitheater best loved by opera buffs, who flock here from all over the world.

INTRODUCTION

by CARLO GRANDE

Italy's unusual shape has always inspired special names. The most lasting name in English–speaking countries is "the boot," but other nations have thought it resembled a cross, or even an oak leaf. They have noted its narrow, elegant length, and have remarked on the intricate coastline with its numerous bays, inlets, and towering cliffs. In reality, Italy is an endless mountain chain stretching from the Alps to the Apennines, as far as Reggio Calabria. Looking at this piece of land from the air, you can imagine it as a hopeful bridge beginning to stretch across the Mediterranean, made up not only of the geography—gulfs, headlands, and estuaries, intensely cultivated mountains and valleys—but also of the Italian people, their generous spirit and their many accomplishments.

Aerial photography provides readers with the unique opportunity to travel high in the skies over this peninsula, to see every nook and cranny of Italy's breathtaking panoramas, cities, fields, and rivers, all reduced to miniatures and spread out like a map before our eyes. The Alps become a maze of valleys and peaks, ridges and waterfalls, lakes, glaciers, and massifs, covered with snow throughout the year—an ancient barrier that was constantly crossed by both travelers and traders through the great Saint Bernard and Brenner passes.

Start with the first dramatic views of Alpine scenery in the Valle d'Aosta. This region is blessed with a singularly harmonious and integrated landscape formed by the great fissure through which the Dorea Baltea River flows. Here, all the side valleys converge with Italy's highest mountains, especially Mont Blanc—over 15,000 feet high.

Nature is certainly awe–inspiring from this bird's–eye view, but so are the works of man. Over the millenia, the mountain slopes have been dotted with hundreds of villages, countless terraces and vineyards, ancient and modern roads and paths. Aosta, the noble capital of the region, is Roman, as its name makes obvious: Augusta Praetoria. It was founded in 25 B.C. by three thousand praetorian guards of the Emperor Octavian Augustus. The square plan of the ancient city, originally a military camp, can be clearly seen from the air—the old walls (many stretches are still standing), a group of monuments including the Arch of Augustus (built to celebrate victory over the Salassi tribe), the remains of the Roman theater and amphitheater, the cathedral, and the collegiate church of Saint Orso (all made from irregularly shaped stones). These features give the viewer a taste of antiquity, as well as of medieval and Renaissance architecture unrivaled in the whole valley.

As the imaginary airborne traveler leaves the area of Mont Blanc and moves toward the lowlands at the foot of the mountains, more than one hundred and thirty castles stretch from Issogne to Fenis, making this area the Italian version of France's Loire valley.

Piedmont means "at the foot of the mountains," a highly suitable name for this region. It is surrounded by the great arc that is formed by the Alps with Monviso (a mountain and symbol that dominates much of the Po Valley) toward the south. It is said that on clear days this mountain can be seen from as far away as the spires of Milan's cathedral.

11 Monte Rosa is one of Europe's loftiest mountains, with the Dufour peak rising to almost 15,000 feet. Spread out from it like a fan are no fewer than four Italian valleys—the Anzasca, Sesia, Ayas, and Gressoney. The Regina Margherita observatory and reserve, installed on its rugged slopes in 1893, is the highest mountain shelter in Europe.

Carlo Grande was born in Turin in 1957. He has written about the ecology and the environment for many Italian and international publications.

12 The elegant city of Turin is situated on the banks of the Po, Italy's longest river. Once, it was the capital of the Duchy of Savoy, and later of the newly united

Kingdom of Italy. In the Parco del Valentino is a medieval-style castle built in the 19th century, resembling those found in the Valle d'Aosta.

12–13 Scattered around the suburbs of Turin are magnificent residences once occupied by the house of Savoy; the castle of Stupinigi is one of the most impressive. It stands in a magnificent park with ancient trees, on the southern

side of the city. Built in 1730 according to a design by Juvarra, it was the hunting lodge of Vittorio Amedeo II. Now housing a museum specializing in art and furniture, it is an exceptional example of Rococo architecture.

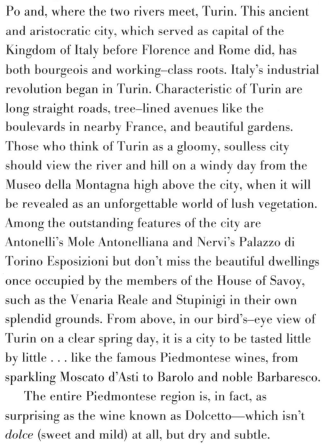

Following the course of the Dora River we come to the Po and, where the two rivers meet, Turin. This ancient and aristocratic city, which served as capital of the Kingdom of Italy before Florence and Rome did, has both bourgeois and working–class roots. Italy's industrial revolution began in Turin. Characteristic of Turin are long straight roads, tree–lined avenues like the boulevards in nearby France, and beautiful gardens. Those who think of Turin as a gloomy, soulless city should view the river and hill on a windy day from the Museo della Montagna high above the city, when it will be revealed as an unforgettable world of lush vegetation. Among the outstanding features of the city are Antonelli's Mole Antonelliana and Nervi's Palazzo di Torino Esposizioni but don't miss the beautiful dwellings once occupied by the members of the House of Savoy, such as the Venaria Reale and Stupinigi in their own splendid grounds. From above, in our bird's–eye view of Turin on a clear spring day, it is a city to be tasted little by little . . . like the famous Piedmontese wines, from sparkling Moscato d'Asti to Barolo and noble Barbaresco.

The entire Piedmontese region is, in fact, as surprising as the wine known as Dolcetto—which isn't *dolce* (sweet and mild) at all, but dry and subtle. The hills in the Langhe and Monferrato areas are an inspiring sight with their mosaic of green and yellow fields, vineyards and villages perched on rocky outcrops *(langhe)* and crisscrossed by roads. Among the delights of the area are truffles, *fritto misto,* a mixed grill including fish, and delightful pastries called *bagna caoda.* From the water, breezes bring the salty tang of sea air and the fragrance of chestnut and yellow broom from the slopes of the Alps to the area. The broom gives an introduction to the vivid colors of coastal towns and villages set in the midst of olive groves and greenhouses vivid with carnations and chrysanthemums.

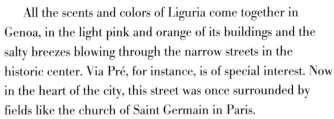

All the scents and colors of Liguria come together in Genoa, in the light pink and orange of its buildings and the salty breezes blowing through the narrow streets in the historic center. Via Pré, for instance, is of special interest. Now in the heart of the city, this street was once surrounded by fields like the church of Saint Germain in Paris.

If we could be carried by the wind it would take us high above the roofs of Genoa. There we would see the labyrinthine alleys and the Via del Campo outside the 12th–century city walls. We would see, close to Porta Soprana, the ivy–covered ruins of what was, tradition says, the home of Christopher Columbus, that man of humble birth who discovered the great American continent. Higher up, forming an amphitheater–like backdrop, are the still–mighty walls of fortresses that defended the city throughout the centuries. Close to the port, which is itself second only to Marseilles in the Mediterranean, is the famous 16th–century Lanterna tower.

The breathtaking natural beauty of the coast provides a perfect setting for Genoa's beauty. From San Remo to as far as Nervi and the Portofino promontory, and down to the Cinque

14 top and 14–15 Along the Ligurian coast, beyond the promontory of Portofino, is a charming little town called Camogli. The seafront is bordered with colorfully painted houses and is awash in glorious seafaring traditions.

14 bottom Nearby Sestri Levante, thirty miles from Genoa, is a popular tourist center.

Terre, this shore enjoys sunshine and warmth throughout the year. Thanks to the surrounding mountains, it is protected from the cold winds coming from the Po Valley. This warmth is captured in the golden–yellow wines produced on the terraces of the Cinque Terre, five hamlets tucked into gaps in the steep cliffs on this stretch of coastline. We can see here, in this unspoiled setting, houses clinging to rocks, narrow passageways, stepped streets, and boats which are beached on tiny pieces of land out of the reach of the sea. Only two of these villages—Monterosso and Riomaggiore—can be reached by car. The other three (Vernazza, Corniglia, and Manarola) can be reached only by foot, boat, or train. For hikers, a footpath to Riomaggiore, located high on the cliffs and named the "via dell'amore" (road of love), has its own special appeal.

Since the 18th century, visitors from all over Europe have been coming to the Cinque Terre. But the many virtues of the Ligurian Riviera—with its woods and gardens, olive trees, palms, and agaves—are special even to the people living in nearby Piedmont and Lombardy. Many come to this area each summer to escape Milan's urban sprawl.

Italy's financial and business capital, Milan can be considered a modern city with an ancient heart. It is not always realized that it is also a city filled with art, from the

magnificent spires atop the Duomo and the masterpieces in
the Brera Art Museum to the La Scala opera house where
such artists as Toscanini and Maria Callas shared their
talents with the world. Milan is also home to Leonardo da
Vinci's painting of the Last Supper.

Leonardo came to Milan at the age of thirty in 1482. In
a letter to Duke Ludovico il Moro he introduced himself as
a designer and builder of war machines, architect, engineer,
hydraulics expert, sculptor, and painter. He was in the
duke's service until the dukedom was invaded by King
Louis XII of France in 1499. Leonardo returned to Milan in
June 1506 and stayed there, protected by the French
governor, until September 1513. He lived in a house at the
East Gate in the parish of Saint Babila.

But the people of Lombard don't vacation only at the
sea. They also love the beautiful blue of Northern Italy's
lakes.

Imagine flying high above these lakes, weightless, in
silence. From space, both astronauts and satellites tell us

that water gives our planet its predominantly blue color,
along with a very special sense of harmony. The water
cycle—the white clouds, the deep blue oceans, the
dazzlingly white glaciers—reveals the vitality of our world.

From the sky over Lake Como we can see the various
parts of this lake, which many believe is the loveliest lake in
the world. There is the "southward–facing" Lecco branch;
the westward branch, whose waters lap first the shores of
Como; then Cernobbio, Moltrasio, Comacina Island, and up
as far as Cadenabbia and Tremezzo. Romantics may
remember a 1930s film in which Greta Garbo suggests to
her lover that they elope to the lakeside village of Tremezzo.
They couldn't choose a lovelier place!

Amid the nearby mountains of Bergamo is the House
of Harlequin, deep in the woods of the Brembana valley.
This house was built in the 15th century and stands watch
over the old road to Bergamo. Tradition says that a servant
of this household, named Arlecchino Batoggi from San
Giovanni Bianco, played himself on the stage.

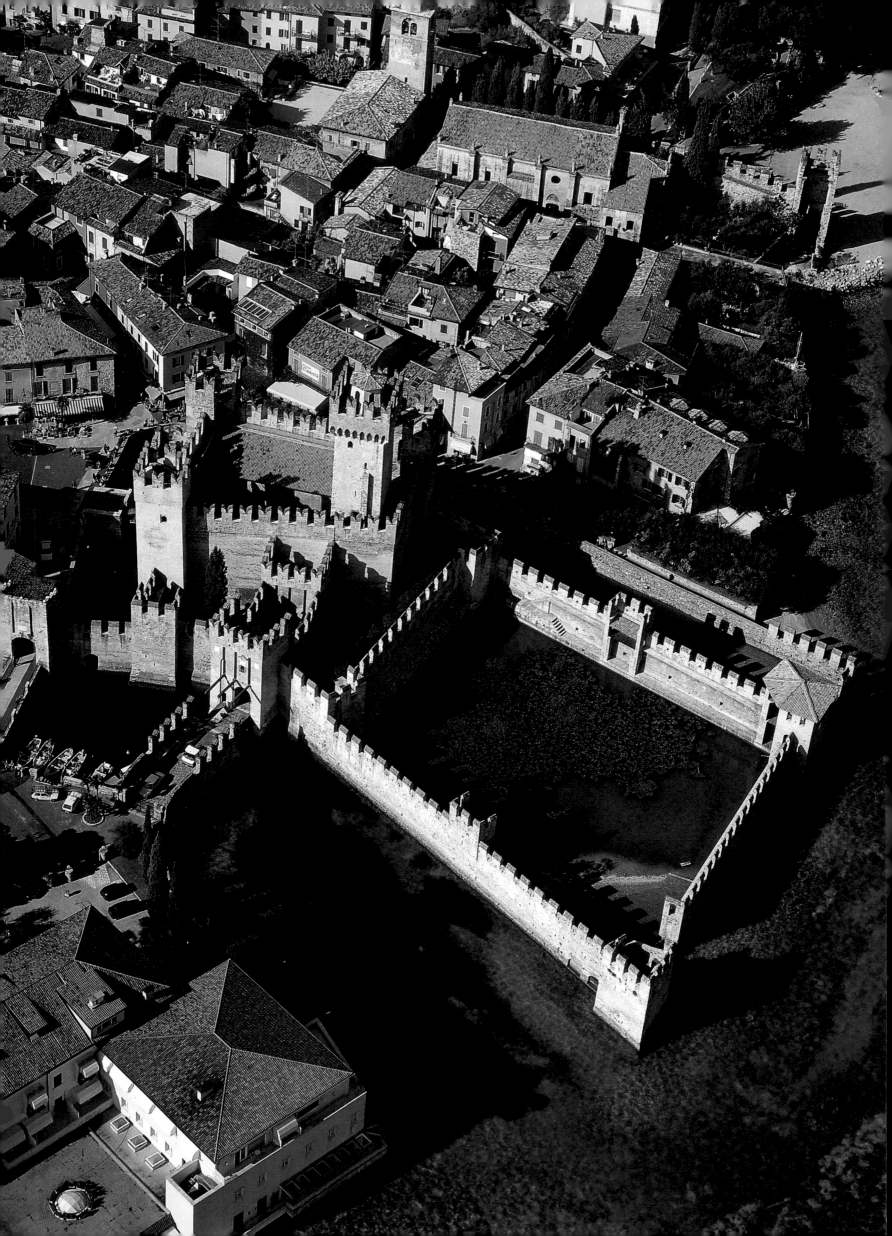

People from Mantua are likely to appreciate the peaceful calm of Lake Garda. Since ancient times, the mild climate here has encouraged the growth of tropical plants such as lemon and olive trees, palms, cedars, and cypresses.

We leave behind the lake's eastern shores and soon are high over Verona. This modern and prosperous town has lost none of its fairy tale elements. The story of Romeo and Juliet remains, making theirs the world's most visited balcony, and the romantic tale of Aida and Radames delights music lovers who crowd into the Arena,

Verona's Roman amphitheater. A home to lovers and opera-lovers alike, Verona has long been an essential part of a trip to Italy, for everyone from Goethe to today's back-packing students. The age-old stones of Verona remind today's visitors that in the Roman era it stood at the crossroads of major trade routes. During the Middle Ages and the Renaissance numerous architectural landmarks were built, including the Arche Scaligere, Saint Zeno, and the Romanesque cathedral.

Along the Brenta we can see numerous centuries-old villas in their silent rural settings . . . they have the solemn, melancholy, but glorious charm of abandoned palaces. The most famous of these are along the river; however, there are many others worth visiting in the provinces of Treviso and Pordenone. There they arise from the beautifully green countryside, with grain, vines, and low-lying towns sprawling out around tall, slender bell-towers.

18 From its headland on Lake Garda, Sirmione radiates charm. The Roman poet Catullus wrote lyrically about its delights. Today, it attracts tourists in hordes, drawn in particular by the Rocca Scaligera, its medieval castle.

19 Visitors flock to the villas along the Brenta canal. Many of the historical dwellings dotted along the canal and amid fields are abandoned, but they are still fascinating testaments to the region's splendid past. The picture at the bottom shows the famous Villa Pisani.

The long shadow of San Marco's Lion reaches these places of ruined splendor, symbolizing the lost civilization of Venice which spread its influence on the mainland only to fade and die. Early in the 16th century, the patrician families of the Republic of Venice abandoned their maritime dominion and turned to the mainland. From Verona's hills and the shores of Lake Garda to the plains of Friuli, these families continued to build stately rural homes for three hundred years, using the great wealth they had accumulated from trading with the Orient.

They commissioned prestigious architects to design and decorate these homes.

At Altivole, near Asolo, stand the remains of the barco—the summer residence of Queen Cornaro. Very little is left today: a tiny church, a building over 100 yards long, and the story of Queen Cornaro. Caterina Cornaro, a Venetian noblewoman, was fourteen years old when she married James II of Lusignano and became Queen of Cyprus, Jerusalem, and Armenia. Forced to abdicate by the Venetians, she was exiled to Asolo. There she held court and was visited by prominent figures in Italian history. Her residence had three rings of walls which enclosed gardens, waterways, and a hunting reserve. Her home became a preeminent site of the early Renaissance period. In 1509 imperial troops of the

League of Cambrai burnt down the barco, but Caterina Cornaro had fled back to Venice. From the barco, the rolling hills of Asolo can be seen in the distant horizon. On a clear day, even distant Monte Grappa can be seen.

Asolo is associated with another famous woman—the actress Eleonora Duse. She loved Asolo for its narrow streets, its gardens, and its peace, and she asked to be buried there in the cemetery of the church of Saint Anna.

Finally we reach Venice, a dream on the water. It is said that this city was built on millions of trees. Larch, pine, walnut, beech, and elm were turned not only into the planks, masts, rudders, oars, and winches of the fleets for this "Most Serene City," but also into the foundations for its great buildings. From Ca'Pesaro to Ca'd'Oro, from the Rialto to Palazzo Grassi, Pietro Aretino said that if the view from his window overlooking the Grand Canal had nourished all of his senses as it nourished his sight, his room would have been paradise—for he could have wished for nothing more.

No other square in the world can rival the Piazza San Marco, which Napoleon described as a splendid drawing room with only the sky worthy of being called its ceiling. Its streets and squares, the treasures in its museums, in the Doges' Palaces, and in San Marco . . . all perpetuate the magic of this enchanted city.

There is no country better than Italy to satisfy a "thirst for landscapes" to be seen from the air. Nevertheless, the scenery we see as we move from Veneto and across the Po Valley is much changed since the early Middle Ages. Then, all Europe was a huge wilderness, with occasional villages lost in the enormous forests. Packs of wolves roamed the streets of Piacenza, Pavia, and Alessandria, and buzzards flew high above the medieval walls.

The Renaissance, a period of great cultural, geographical, and scientific conquest, was also the time when man became the unchallenged lord of the earth. It was in this period that wild animals were slaughtered, until many such animals disappeared (including wolves, beavers, cranes, bears, and countless birds of prey). The effects of the major geographical discoveries were equally dramatic. The expansion of Venice in the 15th century alone marked the end of the few forests that remained after the extensive land clearance of the 11th century.

20 *The very first basilica dedicated to St. Mark was consecrated on the Piazza San Marco in 832 A.D. Today it is the seat of the bishop of Venice, who holds the title of patriarch. On a humbler note, a cattle market was held here even as late as the 1800s. Considered by the Venetians as their city's drawing room, it is a sight not to be missed on even on the shortest trip.*

21 *The Basilica di Santa Maria della Salute was erected in Venice between 1631 and 1687. This colossal form is a prominent feature of the last stretch of the Grand Canal.*

22–23 *Venice is comprised of about a hundred tiny islands emerging from the lagoon. This forms an extremely fragile ecosystem, threatened by both the consequences of man's acts and the rising level of the Adriatic Sea.*

24 Trento, a stark but beautiful city, is encircled by mountains. The hub of urban life is the main square, called the Piazza Duomo, with its Neptune fountain.

25 top Trentino Alto–Adige is border country, with a wealth of castles and fortifications standing guard amid verdant pastures and dark forests, an idyllic realm of serene and picturesque landscapes.

25 bottom La Pusteria is the widest valley of Italy's eastern Alps, between the border chain to the north and the Dolomites to the south.

One area which is still generously endowed with forests is the mountainous Trentino region, situated at the heart of the Alps. This is a magic land, splashed with white, and settled by man even in prehistoric times. The area covers about 2,400 square miles and is centrally placed on one of the main axes that connect the Mediterranean basin and northern Europe. Trentino has been an ideal meeting point of the distinctive cultures of these two worlds since antiquity. It is a dynamic, open frontier which has assimilated values and traditions from both cultures over the centuries.

These influences can be seen in the area's rich heritage of churches, castles, palaces, monuments, and cities both large and small, including Trento, Rovereto, and Riva del Garda. For many years the region has been autonomous at the local government level, and now it even has its own constitution. This autonomy is rooted in its history and the long period when it was ruled by prince–bishops of the Holy Roman Empire. Trento, the capital of the region, was the site of the historic Council of Trent of the Roman Catholic Church. Nature dominates this province—fifty–three percent of its territory is covered by woods and meadows, there are three hundred alpine lakes, and seventeen percent of the territory is part of a strict conservation program, something Trentino is extremely proud of. Agriculture, craft–based activities, and tourism support the local economy.

This is an area of Italy long noted for its spirit of hospitality. The typical dishes in the local cuisine feature wholesome flavors from natural products, grown on hard mountain soil and skillfully prepared. Foods that can be stored through the long winters are important, as are items from the forests (mushrooms, game, salami and many other sausages and cured meats), fish from lakes and rivers, and polenta. And don't forget the assorted cheeses of the region.

Trentino's reputation as a gastronomic capital dates back to the time of the Council of Trent, when the banqueting cardinals enjoyed a variety of simple and elaborate foods. One of the favorite foods from the Council is *gnocchetti verdi*—green dumplings made from bread crumbs, egg, and spinach—popularly known as *strangola preti* or "priest chokers." Because the area is

close to Germany and was dominated by the Habsburgs for a century, Austro–Germanic dishes such as sauerkraut, goulash, and soups made from beans and other vegetables have become part of the cuisine. In desserts and cakes, too, the flavors of Italy meet with the sweetness of the Austrian–Tyrolean style. And no dessert table would be complete without Trentino's Golden Delicious and Rennet apples.

Wine has been produced in Trentino since the Roman era. Hundreds of vineyards, both large and small, turn out famous reds such as Pinot Nero and Merlot and classic white Rieslings. On cold winter days, a glass or two of the local grappa—spirits distilled from mountain herbs—drunk in a warm alpine hut can be a very special experience.

But Trentino is more than just food and drink. It also has its own history, tradition, and customs. To begin to understand the people of the region, visit the Trentino Museum of Customs and Folklore in San Michele d'Adige, north of Trento. It is considered one of the most important museums of its kind in Europe. Trento and Rovereto also have museums with interesting collections of painting, sculpture, and religious and secular architecture. In addition, the castle of Rovereto houses exhibits on the First World War, giving more insights into this remarkable area.

As we pass high over the Po River, we have more chances to admire the amazingly unspoiled areas of Italy, places with no sign of houses, roads, or high tension wires, where the sound of automobile engines is unknown and the only scents in the air are greenery and wild animals. From Monviso to the delta of the river, almost 400 miles, the Po is rich in nature reserves, thick with willows and poplar, and teeming with animal species. One of the loveliest of such places is the Ticino nature reserve, the first river park in Italy. It covers the entire lower course of the river,

from Sesto Calende (where the Ticino leaves Lake Maggiore) to the Becca bridge (where it meets and joins the Po).

The reserve makes the Ticino one of the cleanest and least spoiled rivers of the Po Valley. The Negri woods, for example, near Pavia, are municipally–owned groups of oak, poplar, and alder trees, homes to thousands of birds. At least four species of woodpecker make their homes in these trees, and kingfishers make nests among the roots of trees that

have been blown over in storms. Foxes are often seen here.

As we continue along the Po, down the "boot" of Italy, we reach the cities of the Emilia region. The city of Parma, which was an independent dukedom for three centuries, still has the feeling of a small capital city. It boasts a Romanesque baptistery, the Farnese Theater, and the Duke's palace. The restaurants, pastry shops, and concerts are part of the pleasant lifestyle that is part of this region's heritage. Such easy living is also the tradition in nearby Reggio Emilia, where Italy's national flag (originally the banner of the Cispadane Republic) was born on January 7, 1797. In Ferrara, once the seat of the principality ruled by the House of the Estes, the cathedral, castle, Palazzo dei Diamanti, and long, cobbled streets lined with Renaissance buildings create an unforgettable atmosphere.

But it is in the capital city, Bologna, where we'll find the perfect conjunction of culture and joie de vivre on the Via Emilia. With our bird's–eye view, we see the warm color of its sandstone buildings, the geometric design of its porticos, the Garisenda and Asinelli towers of medieval Bologna still soaring high above the city. Among the city's many other attractions are the oldest university in Europe, the Piazza Maggiore, the Palazzo del Podesta, and San Petronio, one of Italy's finest Gothic churches.

In some respects Bologna can be considered the twin of Florence; located on the other side of the Apennines, this city is just as knowledgeable about good living and good food.

26 The warm red of the city's bricks and sandstone are a reminder of the richness of Bologna, home of Europe's oldest university. Among the monumental landmarks in the old center are the Piazza Maggiore, with the Gothic church of San Petronio (dedicated to Bologna's patron saint), and the Palazzos del Podesta, Communale, and dei Banchi.

27 Two towers are the symbols of the city: the Torre degli Asinelli was built in the first decades of the 12th century; the older Torre della Garisenda was mentioned by Dante in The Inferno.

But Florence, which we are now passing over, is also noted for beautiful, elegant women, glorious shop windows, workshops (it is the craftwork capital of Italy), and cultural events. No other city in the world has so many exceptional art treasures: the masterpieces in the Uffizi galleries would fill a dozen volumes, while the collections in the Palazzo Pitti include priceless works by Raphael, Titian, Tintoretto, and Caravaggio.

Seemingly just out of reach as we wing our way across Florence are Giotto's bell tower (almost 280 feet high) and Brunelleschi's dome on Santa Maria del Fiore, the

baptistery with its exquisite bronze doors, the Palazzo Vecchio, and the many paved streets lined with lofty and monumental buildings. Behind the Palazzo Pitti are the Boboli Gardens, the city's green heart of countless grottoes, fountains, avenues, and walkways. Created four hundred years ago, the gardens offer breathtaking views of the city and luxuriantly growing pines, plane trees, lemon trees, and bay laurel. But the most noticeable trees from the air are the cypresses, pines, and olive trees that surround the glorious white and green marble San Miniato church, adorning the beautiful hill. And then, finally, we see the winding blue line of the Arno river, its width spanned by the 13th-century Ponte Vecchio, haunt of tourists and shoppers and unique symbol of the city.

Actually, every Tuscan landscape is the stuff of dreams—with silver olive groves, long rows of cypress, rolling hills, and pale pink farmhouses reminiscent of Provence. Throughout Tuscany are age-old towns filled with romantic towers, like those throughout the province of Siena. Before we start along the Via Cassia (the road from Fiesole to Rome), following the footsteps of the famous Italian highwayman Ghino di Tacco, we must stop to admire the azure sea that runs along the Tuscan coast, lapping at the shores of Elba. Take time to view a wonderful mosaic of unspoiled scenery accented with long promontories and deep bays, pine trees, vineyards, and prickly pear cactus plants.

Further south, the province of Siena is a marvelous mixture of vineyards, olive groves, houses, and farms. Dark cypresses line up on ridges, while castles and towns perch high up on hilltops, almost glowering at each other over the countryside. As we move along the Via Cassia (parts of which follow old Etruscan trails), we pass through towns such as Radicofani, Poggibonsi, Montalcino, and Montaperti, all centuries old. San Gimignano and Certaldo, the birthplace of Giovanni Boccaccio, still retain their medieval appearance— "erect, on their feet," as Celine said of New York, rather than sprawling across the landscape

horizontally, skirting the sea or bordering a river as so many towns do.

The heart of Certaldo is on a hilltop. It is a maze of passages, ramps, steps, and paved courtyards, with Gothic windows and battlements. Via Boccaccio, made up of red brick and towers, is flanked by the wings of two medieval buildings. After Poggibonsi, we move over the medieval town of Colle di Val d'Elsa. Six miles further south, still on the Via Cassia, we reach the still-intact walls of Monteriggioni, originally a Sienese outpost against Florentine expansion. Carved on one of the fourteen square towers that accent the walls is a quote from Dante's *Inferno*, in which he refers to the town. Monteriggioni still has the charm of an old, unsophisticated rural town, with pink stone houses surrounded by kitchen gardens and olive trees.

Close to Siena lies Montaperti, where one of the major battles of the Middle Ages was fought. On a picturesque hillside, we can see from the air a small pyramid flanked by

a double row of cypresses— a memorial to the bloody defeat of the Florentines by the Tuscan Ghibellines in 1260.

Further south along the Via Cassia, at Buonconvento, another memorial notes a milestone in Dante's career: the death of Emperor Henry VII on August 24, 1313, which dashed the great poet's hopes for future financial support. The small town, still surrounded by parts of its 14th–century walls, lies below the abbey of Monte Oliveto Maggiore. The abbey is surrounded by cypress trees, and its interior is adorned with the splendid frescos of Saint Benedict painted by Luca Signorelli and Sodoma.

Now we leave Buonconvento and move on to Montalcino. This town is the last remnant of a fascinating period of Italian history, during which towns had their freedom to operate independently. Here, in 1555, hundreds of exiles from Siena briefly re–established their Republic after their own town had been taken over by troops belonging to the Habsburg and the Medici families.

28–29 Florence, capital of Tuscany, is one of the cities most generously endowed with works of art. Within its walls, now skirted by wide avenues, the atmosphere is warm and inviting. Its busy streets are lined with elegant shops.

29 top The construction of the cathedral Santa Maria del Fiore was started in 1296. Its dome was designed by Brunelleschi.

29 bottom Crowded with tourists from every corner of the globe, the Piazza della Signoria is dominated by the Palazzo Vecchio and the high arches of the Loggia dei Lanzi. In the background the picture shows Santa Maria Novella; this church was begun by Leon Battista Alberti in the 14th century.

As we leave Montalcino we come to one of the most beautiful Romanesque buildings in Tuscany— the 12th-century abbey of Saint Antimo, standing alone in the center of a rich green valley. The abbey's pure white stone interior is divided into lofty nave and aisle sections by pillars, which are topped with gleaming onyx capitals.

As we return toward the Via Cassia in the direction of San Quirico d'Orcia, we cross the charming small town of Castiglione d'Orcia. This route offers views of Monte Amiata and the valley of the river Orcia, and we can see San Quirico d'Orcia with its splendid medieval sculptures

of the Collegiata. Leaving the Via Cassia we head toward Piensa, a Renaissance gem associated with Enea Silvio Piccolomini, Pope Pius II, who planned to turn his birthplace of Corsignano into an ideal city. The work was never completed, but the splendid piazza with its cathedral and Palazzo Piccolomini are delightful.

Before we look at the enchanting Lake Vico's clear, unpolluted waters, we fly high over upper Lazio and the countryside around Norchia in the province of Viterbo. Here, as far as the eye can see, are fields of sun-baked yellow stubble interspersed with olive groves where crickets sing their monotonous and almost deafening chorus, and occasional patches of barren earth.

Tuscia, or southern Etruria, is another important spot along the route to Rome. Here, hidden in the peaceful countryside, are cemeteries in rocky depressions, part of a silent "lost city." This area's urban centers— Tuscania, Vulci, and Targuinia— were all originally Etruscan and later Roman cities. Now they are rich with towers, Romanesque churches, and fine Renaissance buildings. The dark facades of the 16th-century buildings seem to have the same colors and shapes as the cliffside graves.

Not far from Vulci, excavations are slowly unearthing traces of what was once the largest city-state in southern Etruria. Here we can see the medieval castle of Abbadia and an Etrusco-Roman bridge. This bridge was built between the 4th and 3rd centuries B.C. and spans a deep ravine, 66 feet high over a central arch. On the hillside we can read the history of the area by examining the remains of houses, temples, and a long paved road that eventually disappears into fields, where longhorned cattle now graze.

Tuscania, seated on a bit of porous rock, boasts splendid medieval monuments, including two lovely Romanesque churches from the 8th century, Saint Pietro and Santa Maria Maggiore. The town is still encircled by its walls and towers. In the area many tombs have been discovered, with a series of splendid sarcophagi. The finds from these tombs have been displayed in museums all over Italy— and indeed, throughout the world.

The cemetery of Tarquinia is even more famous; more than six thousand tombs have been unearthed here. The most famous of them (the tombs of the Augurs, the Leopards, and the Lionesses, to mention just a few) are unforgettable, with frescoes painted in basic colors— primarily black, red, and brown. They are among the oldest frescoes in Italy.

30 top Cittadella is a walled village that extends toward the plains of Veneto. Its features include thirty-two towers and four gateways facing the four compass points.

30 bottom The Rocca di Fontanellato, built in the first half of the 15th century, is one of the best preserved castles in Emilia.

31 The hilltop town of San Gimignano has become a symbol of medieval Italy. Within its almost uninterrupted ring of walls (almost two miles long!) are fourteen imposing towers, some 150 feet high.

32 *Assisi is one of the splendors of medieval Italy. This little town is still filled with the spirit of St. Francis, that exemplary figure revered for his humility and his love for all living creatures. Assisi has many splendid monuments, including the Basilica di San Francesco, the Basilica di Santa Chiara, and the cathedral.*

33 *The Basilica di San Francesco, one of the largest sanctuaries of the Christian world, was begun in 1228 at the instigation of Brother Elias of the Franciscan order. He may also have designed the building.*

Slightly further north lies Umbria—the green heart of Italy, often called "the Galilee of Italy." This region is a continuation of Tuscany and a preview of Lazio. Its rolling hills were used as the backdrops for paintings by Raphael and Perugino. Among the medieval towns here are Gubbio, Perugia, Orvieto, Todi, and Assisi (birthplace of Saint Francis, known as "friend to man and beast").

In every corner of every town and village in Umbria, visitors can find some reference to the life of Saint Francis. Monuments to the vitality of the Franciscan order are everywhere; the order spread beyond the borders of Umbria and Italy even during the saint's lifetime. The monuments and sanctuaries are a testimony to the life and work of the *poverello* ("poor one")—however, Umbria's unique verdant landscape offers more insight into the extraordinary figure of this saint. There is an old Italian saying, "If you want to know a poet, you must know about the place he comes from." The saintliness of Francis goes hand–in–hand with his strong poetic sense and great love of nature, as revealed in *The Canticle of the Creatures*, the first and perhaps most outstanding piece of Italian literature.

Along the road from Tarquinia to Viterbo and Lake Vico, we pass Monte Romano and Vetrella, two extremely picturesque villages. Norchia, with its cliffside cemetery, is near Vetrella.

Viterbo is one of the loveliest of all medieval cities, with its surrounding wall still standing. The San Peregrino quarter of this city has been preserved almost intact; here, the spirit of the 13th century still lives. The Piazza del Duomo and the Piazza del Plebiscito are imposing sights, but in many other corners of the town we can find other aspects of centuries long past among the Renaissance buildings and fountains. The beautiful Palazzo dei Papi, close to the cathedral of Saint Lorenzo, was the site of the longest and most famous meeting

in the history of the Roman Catholic Church. The meeting ran from 1268 to 1271—nearly three years—until the commander of the local militia tore off the roof of the meeting hall. He then cut off their food supplies, and the contentious clerics were forced to adjourn!

Just two and a half miles from Viterbo, at Bagnaia, in the splendid Villa Lante's spectacular Italian–style 16th–century gardens, and at Bomarzo, a few miles further north, the Renaissance continues to triumph. The Monster Park of Bomarzo was created by Vicino Orsini in the second half of the 16th century. Huge sculptures of faces, including elephants, lions, bears, ogres, and dragons, make a complex philosophical statement with nature as a backdrop.

The gentle outline of the Cimini hills and the solitary, wooded shores of Lake Vico, at the bottom of a volcanic crater, dominate our view as we move south once again. Much of the surrounding nature reserve, which covers an area of eight thousand acres, consists of centuries–old stands of oak, beech, hornbeam, cerris, and chestnut trees along with large fields planted with walnut trees, one of the area's economic resources. From the bank of "Iacus Ciminus," the walls of the crater offer a truly spectacular sight. Strabo and Cicero say this lake was created when Hercules struck the ground with his club. The villages around the lake, including Ronciglione and Caprarola, are especially impressive. On the eastern slopes of the Cimini hills, presiding over the imposing Renaissance buildings of Caprarola, is the magnificent late 16th–century palace and fortress of Alessandro Farnese, the future Pope Paul III, who convened the Council of Trent.

Sutri, another lively little town built on a spur of rock, has its own special atmosphere. Here, too, architecture from both medieval and Renaissance periods live in perfect harmony. However, the town is of even more ancient origin. It was once part of the territory ruled by Veii, as can be seen from the ancient Etruscan walls and the Roman amphitheater carved from rock and shaded by evergreen oak trees.

From the seacoast town of Civitavecchia, a short sea crossing brings us to the island of Sardinia, home to Italy's most beautiful seascapes. Hundreds of miles of splendid beaches—comparable to those of the Costa Smeralda, the Maddalena archipelago, Stintino, Castelsardo, and Tharros (where the beach is made of fine quartz sand)—are found around this island. The ancient town of Tharros, on the Gulf of Oristano, was founded in 730 B.C. and only abandoned in 1000 A.D. after eighteen glorious centuries. Eighteenth–century archaeologists rushed to its ruins searching for hidden

treasures with so much enthusiasm that it was called "The California of the Mediterranean." Nature reigns in areas such as the Giara di Gesturi, a beautiful plateau where wild Sardinian ponies freely roam among the cork trees. Another natural feature is Lake Mistras, which in antiquity was an important source of fish for people who came to the island from across the seas. The Sardinians themselves at that time were shut away in the mountains of the central Barbagia region. The first immigrants to the island, who apparently came from Spain by way of the Balearic islands, lived in villages of round stone huts built around 1500 B.C. Later, Phoenicians from Tyre and Sidon controlled the island's coasts. Today's Sardinia still has vast wilderness areas such as Sulcis–Iglesiente and Supramonte–Barbagia–Gennargentu. It is also famous for such archeological and artistic splendors as the village of Barumini and the Torralba valley, and Romanesque cathedrals of green and white stone, the most famous of which include Santissma Trinità di Saccargia.

Alghero, an ancient Sardinian fortress city overlooking the sea, has a population where the local language is, surprisingly, Catalan. Cagliarai, the capital, wedged between sea, hills, and inland lagoons, has many restaurants offering the local cuisine based on fish, lamb, kid, pecorino cheese, and almond cakes.

34 top No sea in the world— not even the Caribbean or other parts of the Mediterrean—can rival the translucent waters that lap the shores of Sardinia. The picture shows the barren rock of Caprera.

34 bottom The Stintino promontory is at the tip of the peninsula that forms the western fringe of the great gulf of Asinara, and separates it from the open sea. Close to the glorious beaches of Stintino is the island of Asinara, occupied by a prison.

35 On the island of Caprera, in the Maddalena archipelago, are a famous yachting center and the house where the Italian liberation hero Guiseppe Garibaldi spent his last days.

As we return to the mainland over the coast of Lazio our sights are now set on Rome, capital of Italy and home of the Vatican, built on seven hills, founded by Romulus and raised to greatness under the Emperor Octavian before becoming the capital of Christianity. Rome offers such familiar sights as the Roman Forum, the Trevi Fountain, St. Peter's, and much more. Its historical sites and monuments are known the world over. They are so numerous that visitors can lose themselves among all the cultural and artistic wonders, their imagination recapturing a feeling of the lost

centuries from the view of the ruins that remain.

The Capitoline Hill is the smallest but most famous of Rome's hills, rising only 150 feet above the Roman Forum. High on this hill is the heart of the ancient defensive system, as well as the political hub of the new city. Underground, in catacombs dug from porous rock and running through at least 590 acres of the countryside, is the secret city of the early Christians. Their blood consecrated the arena of the Colosseum, named either because of its size or because of the colossal statue of Nero standing nearby, a tribute to the vainest of emperors. The Colosseum was opened in 80 A.D. and could hold fifty thousand spectators. During the first games, it is said that five thousand ferocious animals were killed there every day for a hundred days. In 249 A.D., as part of the celebrations for the millennium of the foundation of Rome, two thousand gladiators fought in the arena simultaneously. Gladiatorial combat was outlawed by Honorius in 404 A.D.—after the monk Telemachus threw himself into the arena to stop the games and was slain by the crowd.

Since the signing of the Lateran Treaty in 1929, Vatican City has been a sovereign state. It consists of an area of over a hundred acres, which includes St. Peter's Square and Basilica, the apostolic buildings, and the Vatican gardens. Within its walls are such art treasures as the Raphael rooms, the Pinacoteca, and the Sistine Chapel. There are several other outstanding art museums in Rome, too, including the Museo Nazionale di Villa Giulia and the Galleria Doria–Pamphili.

Rome, however, is more than a wonderful fresco of marble architecture, squares (from Santa Maria del Popolo to Campo dei Fiori), and monuments like the Pantheon, Castel Sant'Angelo, and Tinita'dei Monti. Rome also has a superb climate and lush greenery to be found in thousands of gardens and parks such as those at the Villa Borghese.

In Trastevere the simple, delicious, "no frills" aspects of Roman cuisine can be enjoyed in numerous outstanding restaurants. Start with *bruschetta* (crisply toasted bread dipped in olive oil and rubbed with garlic), follow with *spaghetti al'amatriciana* with a dusting of pecorino cheese, and finish up your meal with a dessert of raisins, pine nuts, and bitter chocolate.

The world–renowned Trevi Fountain is a huge baroque scene incorporating Oceanus's chariot on the rocky sea–bed. Tradition demands that, before leaving, we toss a coin into its waters; this ensures that we will someday return to Rome! Then we can safely say farewell to the wonderful sights of historic Rome, and begin our flight above the rich Abruzzo area, which has some of the most beautiful landscapes to be found in all of Italy.

Abruzzo is a place of crafts and trades from the past, of peasants and shepherds who wander through the

mountains with their flocks like bit players in a Mediterranean–style Christmas nativity play. But the area also has fine seacoast cities, such as Pescara. Roaming freely in the Abruzzo National Park (considered by some the loveliest in Italy) are bears, wolves, antelope, deer, beavers, and wild cats; the imperial eagle circles high in the sky above.

The capital town is L'Aquila. Here, standing against the backdrop of the mountains, are such splendid buildings as the Renaissance church of Saint Bernardino; outside the city walls is the Gothic–Romanesque Santa Maria di Collemaggio. Dark forests cover the slopes of the Maiella mountain ridge. Tradition holds that this is a magic mountain, an inaccessible realm of winds which sweep howling through gorges where even wolves and bears cannot penetrate. In this area's villages, life still follows centuries–old customs and superstitions.

36–37 Rome, capital of Italy and the center of Catholicism, is visited every year by many thousands of tourists and pilgrims from all over the world. Among its countless monuments—relics of ancient Rome, and splendid Renaissance and Baroque art and architecture—are such landmarks as St. Peter's Basilica in the heart of Vatican City.

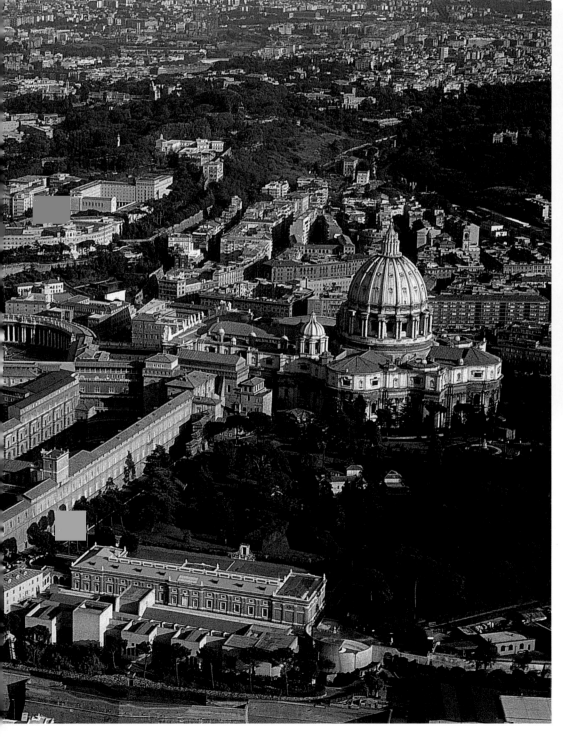

*37 **top** The Trevi Fountain is a stunning expression of Baroque art: a theatrical water show with Oceanus's chariot portrayed in the midst of rocks and cascades, drawn by seahorses and Tritons.*

*37 **bottom** Among the great masterpieces in Rome is the Pantheon, erected in 27 B.C. In the background of the picture can be seen the white marble Altare della Patria (top center) and the Colosseum (top left).*

Leaving the shores of the Adriatic, we cross over to those of the Tyrrhenian Sea. Over five percent of Italy's long coastline has remained completely wild. We leave behind the Royal Palace of Caserta and pass Vesuvius, with the calm blue waters of the Bay of Naples appearing on the horizon. We also see the mixture of narrow lanes, patrician palaces, villas, and other buildings crowding the plain that stretches up to the slopes of the volcano. Naples is a compendium of the light and shade, a metaphorical representative of Italy and the Italians. It combines high spirits with the wisdom of ancient philosophers (its law school is world–famous) and the astuteness typical of

Mediterranean people; it combines the comic levity of its actors with the occasionally melodramatic romanticism of its songs.

The same contradictions can be seen in the chapel of San Gennaro, the city's splendid cathedral. Year after year, the people of Naples wait there for the miracle of the liquefaction of the saint's blood. With great joy, they greet the good news that it has once again liquefied, a mixture of superstition and deep piety. Naples is a gaudily painted scenario that must include the Angevin Fortress and the Teatro San Carlo (a mecca for opera–lovers), the splendid collections of the Museo Archeologico and Capodimonte, the delightfully animated streets of the old city center and the works of art in the 14th–century church of San Lorenzo Maggiore.

The panorama from the hermitage of Camaldoli, a fine viewing point on the very top of the Phlegraean Fields, is a

preview of the vistas that await us along the Amalfi and Positano coasts. These expanses present a thrilling succession of towns and villages that have been clinging to the cliffs throughout the centuries. The cathedral of the former maritime republic of Amalfi (a major naval rival of Genova, Venice, and Pisa) is a masterpiece of Arab–Norman architecture. In almost every season, the islands of Capri and Ischia are splashed with color from luxurious roses, jasmine, bougainvillea, and oleanders.

Under the lofty blue skies that cover the Tyrrehenian Sea we descend to the Cilento coast, which stretches from Paestum to Cape Palinuro, from Agropoli to Marina di Ascea. In ancient times the city of Elea (now Velia) watched the philosopher Zeno develop his subtle arguments while the ashes of Vesuvius covered from view the testimony to Roman civilization hidden, almost intact, in Herculanium and Pompeii.

Flying above, we see the beautiful shores of Campania, which are bathed in light reflected from the sea and filtered by ancient olive trees. Then we soar past towards the wildest parts of the interior of Italy. Basilicata is the land where the courageous fighters of Lucania lived. They had no ambitions to expand their territory, but were strong enough to keep even the ancient Romans at bay. The Greek colony Metapontum was probably defended by soldiers from Lucania; this isn't certain, however, because there were alternating alliances and conflicts with the Greeks during the 4th century B.C. One thing is certain—between 350 and 250 B.C. these people made life very difficult for the settlers of Magna Graecia. Today, the same winds that once filled the sails of the Pythagorean ships sweep the sandy shores of Metapontum.

From the Ionian coast it is easy to move back up to the ancient city of Matera, which is spread out on a rocky spur overlooking a deep ravine. From our viewpoint high above, we can see the vast labyrinth known as the "Sassi," a tangled structure of terraces, stone gardens, balconies, steps, and wells. The wells were part of an ancient water collection system, an ingenious and environmentally friendly scheme that worked from medieval times until it was ended by the industrial revolution.

38 The Royal Palace of Caserta is another glory of the Campania region. Surrounded by a magnificent park, it is the Versailles of the Bourbons.

39 From Sorrento to Positano and Amalfi, the Costiera Amalfitana (the Amalfi Coast) offers a breathtaking drive through villages perched high above the sea.

The Murge plateaus are yellow with grain; beneath them, wrapped in a veil of mystery, lies the necropolis of Gravina di Pugli, an immense pre–Greek city waiting to be unearthed. We are now over Puglia, the agricultural region that fills the heel of Italy's "boot." Puglia includes the Gargano promontory (a peninsula) and the Tavoliere, largest of the few plains of southern Italy. This area is one of endless sandy beaches, clear warm seas, and a high cloudless sky. It seems like a Paradise— but it is one where hard work has been done throughout the centuries. Some of this labor was invested in the spectacular trulli of Alberobello— dwellings made from slabs of limestone built in rows along steep, winding paths. These have become one of the symbols of the region.

Mile after mile of dry stone walls were built with stones removed from the fields, and, amazingly, without mortar. Olive, fig, and almond trees are a typical feature of the countryside around Bari, with its splendid Romanesque cathedral built over the remains of an earlier Byzantine one.

We can see other examples of the region's rich artistic and architectural traditions in Bitonto, in the Basilica di Santa Croce in Lecce and in the cathedral at Trani. The people of Puglia are known primarily for their industriousness, but that is not the limit of their talents. Their outstanding cuisine, rich in vegetables, olive oil, and fish soups, is just one example of their versatility.

Unlike the travelers of the 18th century, who went as far as Naples on their Grand Tours and then rushed immediately to Sicily, we shall visit the rugged beauty of Calabria just beyond the coast. Just below Cape Palinuro and Marina di Ascea, this area is still marvelously unspoiled. It is covered with olive trees, agaves, Aleppo pines, and broom.

40 Alberobello is famous for its trulli houses lining up along narrow, winding lanes. The village itself dates back to antiquity, but the oldest of its houses were built no more than four centuries ago.

41 top Castel del Monte is an architectural masterpiece, an intriguing stone crown built by Frederic II on a barren hilltop, rising to a height of over 600 feet.

41 center bottom Puglia is unrivaled for sunshine and seascapes, a "promised land"

of rocky cliffs, sandy beaches, and extensively cultivated countryside. Its many cities and monuments also attract large groups of tourists.

42–43 Rocca Imperiale, a little town in the interior of Calabria, not far from the border with Basilicata, towers high over the gulf of Taranto and the Ionian Sea. Only a few miles away is the archeological site of Heraclea (modern Policoro), founded in 433 B.C. King Pyrrhus came this way with elephants and mercenaries.

Stretched out along the seacoast and bathed in bright Mediterranean light, Reggio Calabria is now home to the legendary Riace bronzes. Cosenza, where the philosopher Bernardino Telesio once taught, is set in a spectacular ring of hills; there can be found a Gothic cathedral containing the sepulcher of Isabella of Aragon. The whole of Calabria is a revelation, from Stilo, the birthplace of Tommaso Campanella, to the coasts washed by both the Tyrrhenian and Ionian seas. The Aspromonte mountaintop, famous for ancient and heroic battles, is a stunning area that presides over the strait of Messina. The very tip of Italy was the final stopping point for Spartacus and his band of escaping slaves. Unsuccessful in their attempt to cross to Sicily, he and his troops were defeated on the banks of the River Sele by their Roman masters.

For us, the crossing to the Mediterranean's largest island holds no such problems. We can leap over the strait of Messina, just over three miles wide, almost in one jump.

Beneath our gaze we can see the valley of the temples at Agrigento, the sacred precinct at Selinus, the theater at Syracuse, the solitary smooth stone columns on the Segesta hillside. Sicily's Greek heritage alone would be enough to bring legions of tourists to see it, but the island has other attractions. Located on the same latitude as Andalusia and the Peloponnese, its extremely mild winters are a big tourist draw. There is more to do than bask, however; the cultural offerings of the region's architecturally rich cities are also marvelous.

Palermo boasts the splendors of its Arab–Norman past. Once, it was the most densely populated Christian city, second only to Constantinople. The Palatine Chapel, the Norman palace, the grandiose cathedral— where the remains of Emperor Frederick II lie in a red granite tomb— are as memorable as the luxuriant ficus trees in the city's botanical gardens. For a more grisly attraction, visit Piazza Marina, where Joe Petrosino was murdered by the Mafia.

A poet once wrote that Catania is caught in the fragrance of the sea, and the countryside like Venus in her shell. Monreale has a cathedral that almost rivals the mosques of Baghdad and Byzantium. Notice the islands of the archipelagos, from the Lipari to Egadi islands, from Pantelleria to Lampedusa; set in the deep blue sea, with the rich ochre of sun–baked hills accented with hedges of prickly pear cactus, they form a dramatically contrasting beauty.

Unfortunately, in Sicily as in Naples, we find many of the contradictions common to the Bel Paese as a whole. Numerous areas are under threat from unscrupulous developers. Hiding behind the banner of progress, business interests often fail to protect monuments, artwork, and landscapes. Terrible acts of vandalism have been committed throughout Italy by property developers, their conniving cronies, and obliging politicians. Entire coasts and Alps have been covered with ugly concrete buildings, historic towns have been destroyed, inner city blight and soulless sprawling suburbs have been created. Hideous apartment buildings and row houses now blot the same landscapes that were once honored by the world's greatest artists.

And yet, viewed from above, Italy remains a wonderful fresco. Its colors alone— the vivid azure of the seas, the lush green of the forests, the earthy red of its age–old towns— are all that is necessary to understand the nature of true contentment.

44 The Aeolian group is formed of seven islands, but dozens of islets and rocks also surface in this stretch of the Mediterranean. One of the islands with the greatest tourist appeal is Panarea. It has elements of historic interest centered on the remains of a prehistoric settlement from the Bronze Age.

44–45 Syracuse was destroyed by an earthquake in the 17th century. Sicily's most powerful city in ancient times (described by such historians as Thucydides), today it still has countless Baroque buildings such as the cathedral, which incorporates truly ancient columns.

45 top Lampedusa is the best known island of the Pelagic group, off the southern shores of Sicily towards Tunisia. Much of the coast of this mainly rocky island, with its sparse vegetation, is fringed with steep cliffs dropping straight to the sea.

45 bottom After Malta, Pantelleria is the second largest island of the southwest Mediterrean. Once occupied by Arabs and Normans, it has distinctive stone houses known as dammusi.

45

SPARKLING LAKES, ENCHANTING COUNTRYSIDES

46 *Tucked between sparsely populated, high, wooded hills is Lake Orta (also called Cusio). South of Omegna, it is situated only a few miles from Lake Maggiore.*

47 *Isola San Giulio, in the Cusio region, is the most popular place for tourists. They reach the little island by boat to visit the medieval basilica still standing there.*

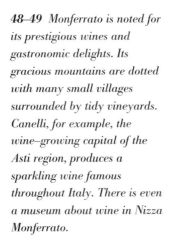

48–49 Monferrato is noted for its prestigious wines and gastronomic delights. Its gracious mountains are dotted with many small villages surrounded by tidy vineyards. Canelli, for example, the wine–growing capital of the Asti region, produces a sparkling wine famous throughout Italy. There is even a museum about wine in Nizza Monferrato.

50–51 The landscape of the Apennines of Liguria, lightly covered with snow, reveals the winding fields of the valley. Walnut trees dominate the dense woods. In the past, this region was ruled by the feudal families of Genoa: first the Fieschi, then the Doria.

52 *The river Ticino (150 miles long) borders both woody areas and cultivated fields along its winding course.*

52–53 *The Alps, partly covered with snow, form the background to the Lombardy plain, a fertile land intensively cultivated through the ages. Agriculture has guaranteed the accumulation of wealth later used in industry. Rice, sugar beets, and sweet corn are produced in this area.*

54-55 *The landscape of the Lombardy countryside varies not only according to the shape of the region and its vegetation but also according to certain unusual atmospheric phenomena. Here in the valley of northern Lombardy, the cold* *and humid climate—lasting six months out of the year— can create wonderful scenic effects. In these pictures, the morning fog rises slowly from the hills which surround Varese, creating a dreamlike landscape.*

56–57 Lake Maggiore lies in a deep fold carved by glaciers at the head of the Ticino valley. Vegetation flourishes on the surrounding land. The shores of the lake, with their bays and creeks, are accented with modern and ancient buildings and magnificent villages, built by the aristocracy and the wealthy from the mid–19th century onwards.

58–59 The Lake of Lugano (or Ceresio) laps along a short stretch of the border between Lombardy and Switzerland, north of the city of Varese.

60–61 *Lake Garda is popular, particularly at its best–known resorts, such as Sirmione with its majestic castle stretching out into the sea.*

61 *Sirmione, a thermal spa, stands on a promontory. On the headland are the remains of a Roman villa, known as the "Grotto di Catullo"—the cave of Catullus, the famous Latin love-poet.*

62 *The island of Garda is a splendid green garden in the blue of the lake waters. Lake Garda owes its origins to the stone deposits left by a glacier, which formed a barrier across the plain at the height of* *present–day Desenzano. The basin created then filled with water. This explains the shape of the lake. In the north, it is long and narrow with rocky cliffs hugging the shoreline like a Nordic fjord.*

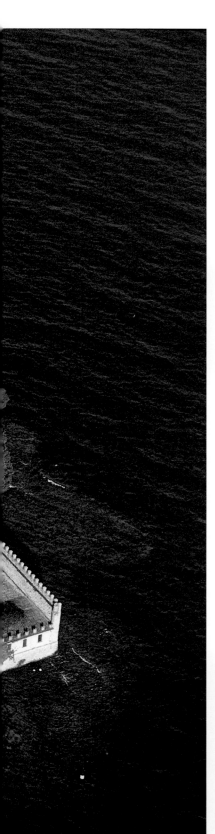

63 *The island of Loreto is like a piece of jade dropped in Lake Iseo. Also known as "Sebino," this lake lies at the entrance to the Valcamonica.*

It charms visitors with its green, lush shores and its azure blue waters. Vegetation flourishes thanks to the mild climate of these shores.

64–65 *Thirty miles from Ferrara, the little town of Comacchio developed on a cluster of thirteen tiny islands in the midst of lagoons, called the Valli di Comacchio. It remained isolated by water until 1821, but now it can be reached and visited easily by bridges. These lagoons and the entire delta of the Po River are visited by many nature–lovers, particularly bird watchers.*

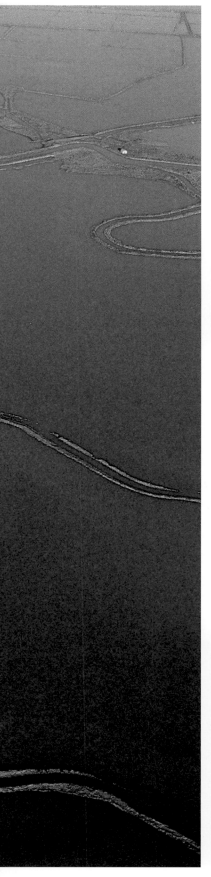

66–67 *A large–scale land reclamation scheme, started in the 1950s, drained thousands of acres of marshes in the Valli di Comacchio, but not without loud protests voiced in favor of these wetlands, home to many species of birds and fish.*

Countless bridges were demolished and canals covered. The local population, once mostly fishermen (eels were their most important catch), is now employed on the land and in the now–thriving tourist resorts along the coast.

67 *The picture shows a detail of the Candiano canal with fishermen in boats arranging their characteristic nets. North of the Candiano canal stands the district called Porto Corsini. Near the mouth of this canal is Marina di Ravenna, not far from the well–known pine forest.*

68–69 *The castle of Torre Chiara is an imposing and spectacular building erected by Pier Maria Rossi between 1448 and 1460. It has three rings of walls and large corner towers. Visitors can admire a series of elegantly decorated rooms, including the so–called Juggler's Room and the "golden chamber," with frescoes by Benedetto Bembo. A countryside colored in thousands of hues of green and contrasting fields completes the landscape.*

70–71 *Monteriggioni, situated only a few miles from Siena amid charming hills covered with vineyards, is an appealing little town surrounded by beautifully preserved medieval walls.*

71 top *The Garfagnana region, in Tuscany, is made up of the upper and central valley of the Serchio, wedged between the Tuscan–Emilian Apennines, Apuan Alps, and the Valle della Lima.*

71 bottom *The Chianti region of Tuscany is well known for the precious wine it produces, as well as for its pleasant landscape.*

74–75 *In the countryside of Sicily—a hilly, mainly mountainous island—the terrain has the colors of the desert, all in hues of yellow, mustard, ochre, and brown.*

76 *Winding roads, rows of olive or almond trees, and stone walls break up the Sicilian countryside. Even in winter, the region never really suffers from cold weather.*

77 *Castelbuono, in the province of Palermo, is a vacation resort dropped into a landscape of olive and almond trees on the Madonie hills. The photograph shows the unusual topography of the small village perched below the ruins of the castle.*

78–79 *One of the places in Italy where salt is produced is the province of Trapani. A dazzling feature of the landscape immediately to the north are saline deposits that seem to be planning an attack on the city.*

Cities: Living Museums of Art and History

Milan

80 The Arco della Pace, shown from the side in the photograph, rises imposingly at the far end of Parco Sempione, the huge park at the rear of the Castello Sforzesco.

81 The cathedral in Milan, Italy's finest example of Gothic architecture, was begun by Gian Galeazzo Visconti in 1386. Its face was not completed until the early 1800s, at the urging of Napoleon.

On its roof are over one hundred and thirty spires, as well as the central lantern with a gilded statue of the Virgin Mary on top. In the crypt is a silver urn containing the remains of St. Carlo Borromeo.

82–83 *Erected over an existing fortress by Francesco Sforza in 1450, the Castello Sforzesco has been altered many times through the centuries by different hands.*

83 top *The Basilica di Sant'Ambrogio, one of the most beloved symbols of Milan, was built in Romanesque style at the end of the 4th century. In its crypt rests the body of the city's patron saint.*

83 bottom *The troubled history of Milan is mirrored in its architecture and changing skyline. Now, next to ancient monuments, giddy skyscrapers rise at the heart of financial and commercial Milan.*

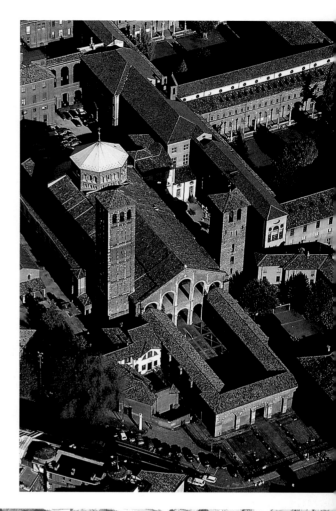

84-85 *As the sun starts to set over Milan, the city presents a deeply romantic sight. The Gothic silhouette of the cathedral and the handsome palazzi around it are brilliantly illuminated.*

86 Pavia, once capital of the Lombards, stretches along the banks of the Ticino river. This photograph shows two of the many famous towers embellishing the city and some minor courtyards of the university. In the area around Pavia is the celebrated Charterhouse, founded in 1396 by Gian Galeazzo Visconti.

87 top Vigevano, a small Lombardy town well–known for the manufacture of shoes, has a superb historical center. Its heart, the Piazza Ducale, together with the adjoining Castello Visconti–Sforza, is a splendid example of Renaissance art.

87 bottom The Ponte Coperto of Pavia crosses the Ticino river, linking the Borgo Ticino district with the rest of the town. It is a reconstruction of a 14th–century bridge destroyed in World War II. The cathedral can be seen on the left–hand side near Strada Nuova, the natural continuation of the bridge toward the castle.

CITIES OF THE LOMBARD REGION

88–89 *The hilltop town of Bergamo, lying more than three hundred feet above the entrance to the Val Brembana and to the Val Seriana, is still surrounded by 16th–century walls. At its heart is the Piazza Vecchia and the Palazzo della Ragione, Italy's oldest town hall.*

89 top Monza, an industrial town on the fringe of Brianza, is known chiefly for the Autodrome, where the Italian Formula One Grand Prix takes place. However, the town also has a picturesque historic center where visitors can see a splendid cathedral. It was built by Theodolinda in the 6th century, but was rebuilt in Gothic style in the 13th and 14th centuries.

89 bottom The hillside of Sacro Monte, where the sanctuary of Santa Maria del Monte stands, commands breathtaking views over Varese and the lakes.

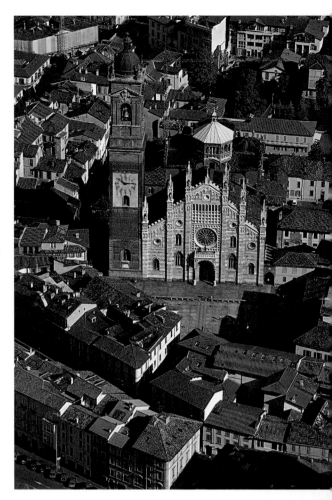

TURIN

90 left The Po River cuts across the city of Turin a few steps from the historic center. On one side is Vittorio Veneto square, not far from the Mole Antonelliana; on the other side is the church of the Gran Madre, majestically facing the river and the square.

90 top right The aristocratic San Carlo Square— "Turin's drawing room"—is bordered by the baroque churches of San Carlo and Santa Cecilia.

Baroque is the prevailing style of the center's most prominent monuments. The capital of Piedmont, which was Italy's first capital from 1861 to 1865, has Roman origins but lived its golden age during the Risorgimento, Italy's struggle for independence.

90 right Turin's symbolic center is the Mole Antonelliana, which offers scenic views over the city, the river, the hill, and the Alps.

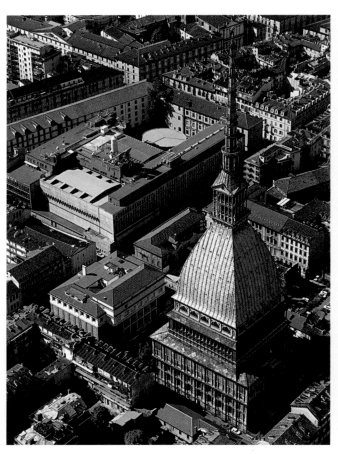

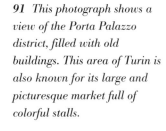

91 This photograph shows a view of the Porta Palazzo district, filled with old buildings. This area of Turin is also known for its large and picturesque market full of colorful stalls.

92-93 *The medieval heart of Genoa hugs the old port area, a labyrinth of narrow alleys lined with tall buildings. The Piazza San Matteo is also medieval with houses built by the Doria family. Nearby are many monumental squares and streets like Via Garibaldi, admired for its 16th- and 17th-century palaces. The symbol of Genoa is the Lanterna, its oldest lighthouse.*

92 bottom *This photo shows Piazza della Vittoria, which is characterized by broad, regular geometric spaces. Within it stands the Arco Trionfale.*

93 bottom left *In the northwestern outskirts of the city rises the imposing bulk of the 17th–century Albergo dei Poveri.*

93 top right *This photo shows Palazzo Reale from an unusual viewpoint. A beautiful hanging garden embellishes the facade.*

93 bottom right *A stone's throw from Piazzale San Benigno stands the symbol of Genoa: the Lanterna, the city's oldest beacon. Constructed in 1547, its light is visible up to thirty miles from the coast*

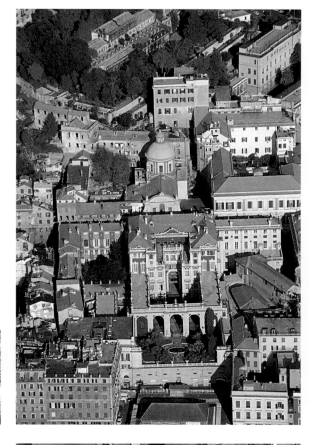

94–95 *Genoa, Italy's foremost port, was once a maritime republic. At that time it owed much of its power to ship–owning families, including the Dorias. In the 19th century, the city was a base for the Risorgimento independence movement, under the leadership of Giuseppe Mazzini.*

GENOA

VERONA

96–97 *The castle at Verona, a massive and wonderfully preserved Renaissance building, overlooks the Adige River. Some of the glorious legacy of Rome can still be seen in Verona—most notably the Arena, but also the Teatro Romano, the Porta dei Borsari, and the Arco di Gavi. In the older part of the city, which is crossed by the Adige River, are a series of squares connected by narrow streets and alleys. Among the most appealing are the Piazza della Erba, built on the site of the ancient Roman forum, and the Piazza dei Signori.*

Veneto and Padua

98 top left *The old center of Bassano del Grappa, a small town in the province of Veneto, is famous for its meandering, arcade–lined streets and the covered wooden bridge that straddles the Brenta River.*

98 bottom left *Marostica nestles on a hillside, at the foot of the upland plateau on which Asiago stands. The town is encircled by medieval walls. Every other year, a costumed human chess game is held in the Piazza Castello, the main square.*

98 right *Vicenza, another Veneto town of Roman origin, reveals the influence of nearby Venice. Many of its magnificent palazzi were designed by Palladio, who died here in 1580.*

99 *The Basilica di Sant'Antonio da Padova in Padua is among the most celebrated churches in Italy. However, Padua is also famous for the Cappella degli Scrovegni, which is adorned with frescoes by Giotto.*

VENICE

100 top *Bisecting the city, the Grand Canal bustles with both water buses and gondolas. It is crossed by many bridges, among which are the Rialto and the Sospiri (shown here).*

100 bottom *Among the most splendid sights of Venice is the Piazza San Marco, with the Basilica di San Marco and the Palazzo Ducale.*

101 *Venice stands amid the waters of the Venetian lagoon, between the mainland and the open sea. It grew on a group of 118 tiny islands, now crossed by 150 canals and 400 bridges. The most famous canal is the Grand Canal (in the photo).*

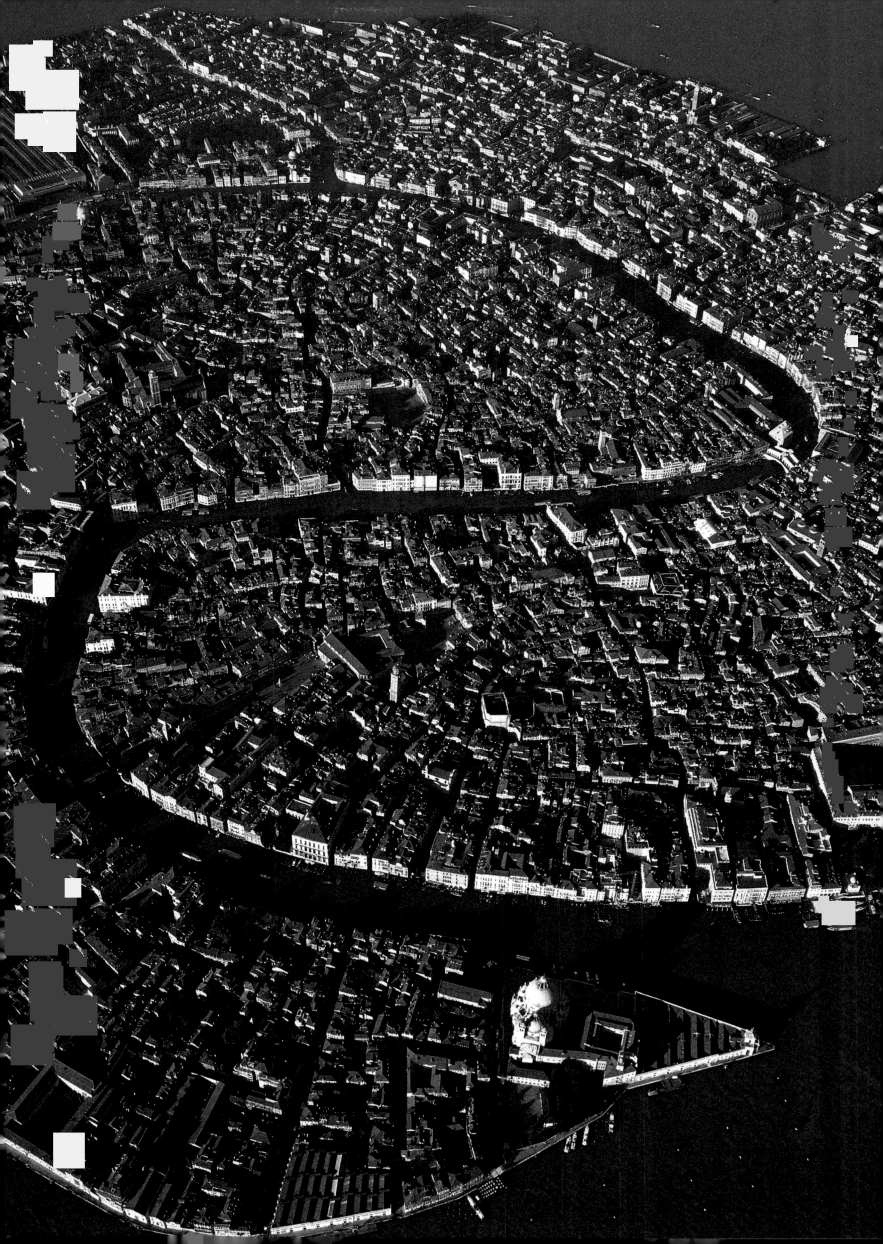

102 Soaring above the Piazza San Marco is the bell tower of St. Mark's, which boasts stunning medieval mosaics among its many treasures.

103 top The splendid Venetian church of Santa Maria della Salute, a masterpiece attributed to Longhena, has imposing entrance steps, a huge cupola, and buttresses accented by scrolls.

103 bottom The church of San Giorgio Maggiore was built around the Benedictine monastery, which was was developed on the island as early as the 10th century. After a period of decline in the early 1800s—when San Giorgio was used as a free port and artillery garrison—its future was totally changed in 1951 by Vittorio Cini, who turned the island into a cultural foundation to honor his son Giorgio.

104–105 The unique physical characteristics of Venice, together with outstanding architecture and countless artworks, have made it one of the world's most beautiful and famous cities.

106 *There are numerous islands dotted about the lagoon. The Lido is an elegant beach resort and venue of an important Film Festival. Murano (in the photo) consists of five islands and is famous for glass-making. San Francesco del Deserto is a tiny and solitary island, and Torcello is north of the lagoon.*

107 *San Francesco del Deserto is one of the most appealing islands of the Venetian lagoon: a solitary spot of land covered with cypress trees.*

108–109 *Five miles away from Venice, the fishing island of Burano is known for its brightly painted houses and lace-making.*

110 top left *Modena was once the capital of an Este duchy. Its cathedral is one of the finest Romanesque churches in Italy.*

110 bottom left *The old center of Parma boasts many fine buildings, some of which are enriched by beautiful arcades. The city is famous for its gastronomic specialties, particularly Parmesan cheese and raw Parma ham.*

110 top right *Ferrara's period of greatest prosperity occured during the Renaissance. Its fortunes were linked with those of the house of Este.*

CITIES OF EMILIA-ROMAGNA

110 bottom right and 111 *Founded as a Roman colony, Reggio Emilia—like Modena—later belonged to territories controlled by the dukes of Este. The typical Renaissance architecture characterizing many of its palaces reveals the glories of that age.*

112–113 *Bologna, of Etruscan origin, is a leading center of industry and trade; with the oldest university in Europe, it is also of notable cultural importance. Focal points of life in the old city are the Piazza Maggiore, with the church of San Petronio, and the Piazza Nettuno, where visitors can see the celebrated 16th century fountain by Gianbolonga. Together with the Piazza di Porta Ravegnana, home of the two leaning towers, these landmark sites form a harmonious ensemble.*

FLORENCE

115 *Piazza San Giovanni houses two of the most remarkable jewels of Italian architecture. The Duomo, the undisputed masterpiece of Italian Gothic, was started in 1296 and was finished 150 years later; the Baptistery was rebuilt on Roman foundations and is striking in its use of a regular octagonal plan and contrasting white and green marble.*

116–117 *Florence has two prevailing colors: gray, seen in the stone of its noble streets and monuments, and red, for the bricks and tiles of its palazzi. The streets that flank the Arno are now promenades, while the church of San Miniato offers wonderful views over the city and green hills beyond.*

114 top *The dome topping the Duomo of Florence is without question one of the symbols of the city. Filippo Brunelleschi worked on this architectural wonder for sixteen years during the first half of the 16th century.*

114 bottom *Alongside Brunelleschi's unmistakable dome rises Giotto's Tower, or the Campanile, in all its splendor. Begun by Giotto, the Campanile was eventually completed to his design by Andrea Pisano and Francesco Talenti. Lower down appears Palazzo Vecchio facing onto the celebrated Piazza della Signoria.*

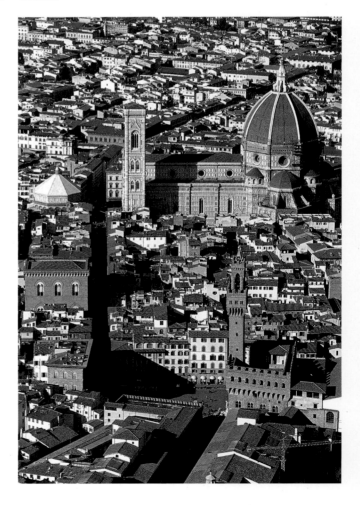

119 *The Arno flows between walled embankments. Before these were reinforced (a plan not yet totally completed), the city was periodically hit by disastrous floods. Running* *along the eastern side of the Ponte Vecchio, above the shops, is the elevated Corridoio Vasariano, a covered walkway linking the Uffizi with the Palazzo Pitti.*

118 top *The Ponte Vecchio, rebuilt in 1345, is perhaps the best known landmark in Florence. The old bridge is not just a means of crossing the Arno, it is a showpiece of commerce and artistry. Strollers who linger awhile are also offered a magnificent view.*

118 bottom *The Palazzo Vecchio—the "Old Palace," also called the Palazzo della Signoria—is traditionally attributed to Arnolfo di Cambio. It stands about halfway between the Duomo and the Arno, with its clock tower rising above the surrounding buildings.*

PISA

120–121 Pisa owes its worldwide fame to the Leaning Tower, but the nearby cathedral and baptistery are also stunning sights to be enjoyed in the Piazza dei Miracoli. The shapes of these edifices are highlighted by rows of contrasting marble.

SIENA

122–123 *The historic center of Siena, built on three hills in the heart of Tuscany, offers some unique treasures. These include the medieval Piazza del Campo, where the Palio race takes place. This square is dominated by the magnificent Palazzo Pubblico and by the cathedral with its Romanesque campanile.*

Lucca

125 top *In the early 19th century, the wide embankment on the walls of Lucca was planted with trees and turned into an elevated promenade, crowned by verdant grass. The tree–lined promenade now marks a border between the old and the new city.*

125 bottom *One of the splendors of Lucca is the church of San Michele. Beneath a huge statue of the saint, the church is adorned with beautiful inlaid marble and four tiers of carved and twisted columns.*

124 *During the last century, rundown buildings in the Roman amphitheater were cleared. Only those clinging to the long–buried steps were left standing. Today, the Piazza del Mercato once again reveals the splendid original shape of the arena.*

126–127 Perugia, capital of Umbria, was originally an Etruscan settlement, later conquered by the Romans. Perched high on a hill offering splendid vistas over the Tiber valley, the old city center still looks typically medieval.

CITIES OF UMBRIA

127 top *Orvieto, built on a plateau of volcanic rock, is home to a cathedral that many consider one of Italy's finest Gothic buildings. However, the Etruscan town has other interesting sights to reveal, particularly in the oldest quarter.*

127 bottom *Spoleto is rich in historical and artistic evidence of the Roman, medieval, and Renaissance eras. It features a marvelous cathedral consecrated in the 12th century, with a campanile built of stones taken from Roman buildings.*

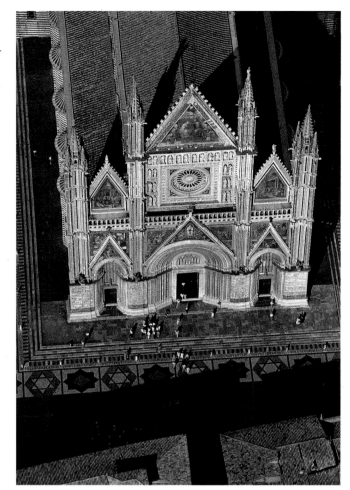

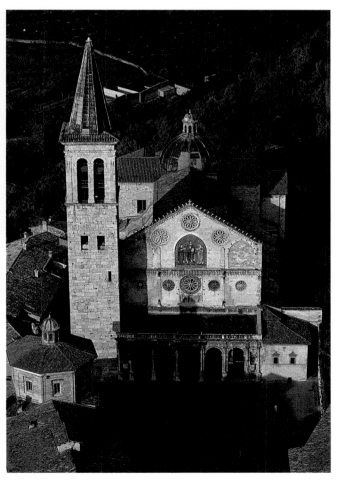

128 top *The Piazza del Popolo is one of Rome's many hundreds of beautiful squares. At the center of its distinctive oval form is an Egyptian obelisk.*

128 *Occupying a strip of land in a bend in the river, Tiber Island is a picturesque part of the urban landscape. Its ship–shaped form was created in travertine stone during the imperial era. The island is linked to the left bank by the Ponte Fabricio, the oldest bridge in Rome after the Ponte Milvio in the outskirts of the city.*

ROME

129 *Not even a view of Rome taken from high above can capture all the most prominent landmarks of Italy's capital, founded—according to tradition—on April 21, 754 B.C.*

130–131 *In urban Rome— that is, between the Foro Italico (upstream) and San Paolo Fuori le Mura (downstream)— the Tiber is spanned by twenty–two bridges, including Ponte Vittorio Emanuele II and Ponte Sant'Angelo, built by Hadrian to provide access to his mausoleum. For centuries, the latter bridge was the main link between the Vatican and the city center.*

132 bottom left The Fontana della Barcaccia, designed by Bernini in the 17th century, looks like an open eye at the center of the Piazza di Spagna.

132 top The lovely Baroque Piazza Navona reflects the oval shape and size of a stadium built by Domitian on this same site. At its center stands Bernini's fountain, the Fontana dei Fiumi.

132 bottom right With the Spanish Steps leading to the Piazza di Spagna and Via Condotti, the Trinita dei Monti offers an exceptionally picturesque sight.

133 The Victor Emmanuel Monument, built in honor of Victor Emmanuel II, symbolizes national unity and offers an ideal backdrop for state ceremonies. Its size and white limestone structure make it particularly outstanding.

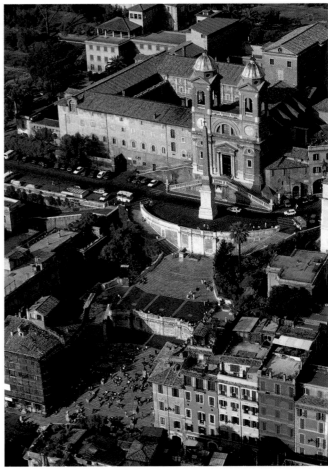

134 The Colosseum (also known as the Flavian Amphitheater) is the best known of the Roman monuments, a true symbol of the city.

135 The dominating landmarks of Vatican City are Saint Peter's Square, designed by Bernini as one of the most grandiose spaces in the world, and St. Peter's, the largest church in all of Christianity.

136–137 Founded by Greek colonists, Naples later fell to the Romans. The city has been called "Parthenope" at various times in the past, a name said to honor a mermaid around whose tomb the city developed. The monumental center of *Naples hinges around the Piazza del Plebiscito, semicircular in shape and closed on one side by the Palazzo Reale. Behind the palace is Castel Nuovo, the fortress also known as the Maschio Angioino.*

138–139 Naples was rediscovered in the 18th century by Grand Tour travelers who were visiting the ruins of Pompeii and Herculaneum. Today, the splendid bay, the castle–topped *hill of Capodimonte, the Museo Archeologico Nazionale (one of the world's most important museums), and many wonderful Baroque churches continue to attract crowds of international visitors to the city.*

140–141 *Pompeii is spectacular from any viewpoint, chiefly because of its size; it was an exceptionally large town for its time. Other sources of delight are its state of preservation and the countless items of artistic, historic, and cultural interest revealed at every turn. The tragic eruption of Mount Vesuvius—which also destroyed Herculaneum and Stabiae—occurred in August of 79 A.D. The city was buried beneath a layer of volcanic debris eighteen feet deep.*

142–143 *In the town of Bari, wonderful buildings like the massive castle shown here are preserved. According to legend, Bari was a settlement of Illyrian origin, later colonized by the Greeks. It was important during the era of Byzantine rule and flourished under the Normans in the Middle Ages. Today it is one of the biggest cities in southern Italy, with a busy port and thriving industrial and trade activities, such as the Fiera del Levante.*

144–145 *Founded by the Phoenicians, Palermo was later conquered by the Romans and ruled by Saracens. The cathedral of Monreale, near Palermo, offers panoramic views of the city and of Mondello beach, not to be missed.*

PALERMO

144 top *This picture shows the Palazzo dei Normanni, an ancient Arab fortress turned into a splendid palace. It was once the political and administrative center of the Norman kingdom.*

145 *The Teatro Massimo (shown in the top photograph) is one of the most characteristic buildings in Palermo. The historic center is dotted with such picturesque squares as the one called della vergogna—"shameful"—because of its nude statues.*

146 top right *Trapani was originally a cluster of rocks and islands, but had become a prosperous trade center by the time it was occupied by the Greeks. Its port became an important Carthaginian naval base.*

146 bottom right *Catania, with Mount Etna dominating its horizon, is Sicily's second largest city. In 1693 it was almost entirely wiped out by an earthquake.*

147 *With evidence of human presence as early as the third millennium B.C., Ragusa has extremely ancient origins. It was eventually settled by Sicilians who were fleeing the colonization of the coasts for the still–secure inland.*

146 left *Messina, gateway to Sicily, was the first Sicilian city to be overrun by the Romans in 263 B.C. Through the centuries, numerous restorations have changed the urban landscape; the city has been ravaged by disastrous earthquakes and World War II air raids.*

THE FORCES OF NATURE

148-149 Monviso, the "Stone King," stands 12,000 feet high, towering over the plains of Piedmont. On clear days, it is visible in far-off Lombardy. This impressive granite mountain was first conquered by an Englishman, William Matthews, on August 30, 1861. The source of the Po River is in the vast plateau that lies at the foot of the mountain, almost 7,000 feet above sea level.

150 *The Valle d'Aosta is a land of rugged but majestic beauty, with a line-up of mountains to arouse the envy of any other mountainous region of Europe. Towering over its valleys are several of the highest peaks on the continent. Stretching from Mont Blanc to the Matterhorn and Monte Rosa is an awesome mosaic of rocky chains and spectacular glaciers.*

151 *The extremely beautiful panorama offered by the summit of Mont Blanc is unique. From this "roof of Europe," there are breathtaking views over the Haute Savoie, as well as other groups of the Italian Alps.*

152-153 *Much of the prosperity enjoyed in the Valle d'Aosta region comes, directly or indirectly, from its mountains. Tourism, in the form of vacationers and day tourists, has made many villages world-famous. Places like Breuil-Cervinia, Champoluc, Courmayeur, Cogne, Gressoney-la-Trinite, and Saint Vincent have been transformed from mountain villages into popular year-round resorts for walkers and skiers.*

154-155 *Mont Blanc, Europe's highest mountain at over 15,000 feet, is called "the king of the Alps." It is formed of dozens of peaks of various heights. Its walls, less steep on the French side, are rugged and razor-sharp on the Italian side.*

156-157 *The race to conquer Mont Blanc began in the 18th century. In 1786, French climbers were the first to reach the summit. Today, many roped parties venture onto the walls and glaciers of the mountaintop every year, convinced that these well-tried routes are an excellent place for training.*

158-159 *Along the cliff faces of Mont Blanc, gullies of ice, perpendicular walls, and challenging ridges test even the most experienced climbers, who are rewarded with breathtakingly spectacular sights.*

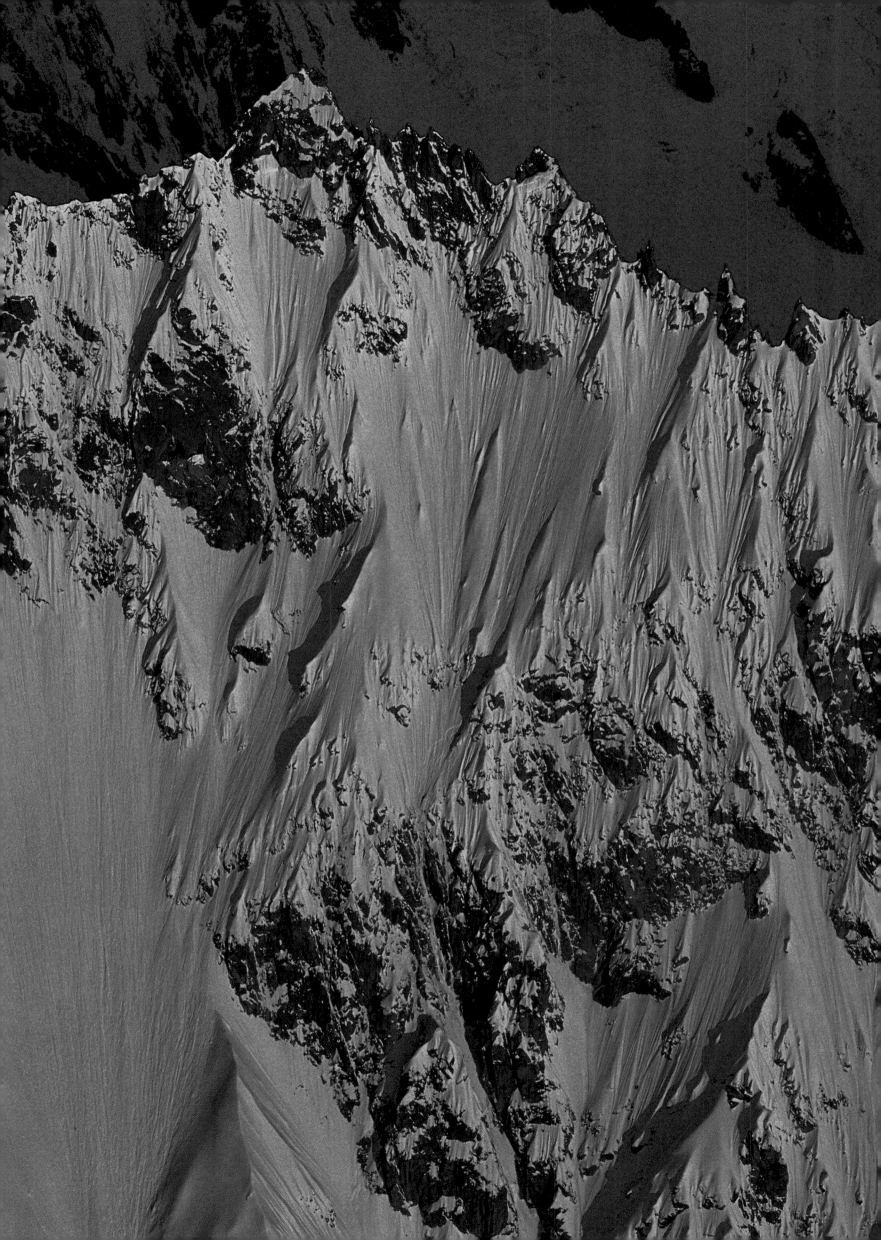

160-161 *The Aiguille du Geant, soaring over 13,000 feet, is not the very summit of the Mont Blanc mountain ridge, but it is certainly one of the most famous peaks. This granite pyramid stands over the glaciers, ridges, and gullies of the tallest mountain in Europe. Its unmistakable mass is surrounded by some of the world's most celebrated peaks: Les Grandes Jorasses, Aiguille du Midi, and Aiguille des Glaciers. The toothy ridges typical of this side of Mont Blanc (splendidly exemplified by the Aiguille du Geant) are created by the wearing action of rain and wind, together with the vertical stratification of the granite.*

162-163 *Viewed from the Aiguille du Geant, Mont Blanc looks like a huge sleeping giant painted pink by the light of the sunset.*

164 Monte Rosa offers splendid views from both the Valle d'Aosta and the Valsesia, dotted with resorts which are not yet ruined by tourism. The Valsesia side of Monte Rosa Alagna is home to a community where people wear traditional costumes.

165 The Matterhorn is a distinctive granite pyramid, rising to over 14,000 feet. Its unmistakable triangular profile dominates the valley of Valtournenche. Exceptionally dramatic views are offered both from the Plateau Rosa and from the tiny, pine-swathed Lago Blu (Blue Lake) of the upper valley.

166-167 Beneath the snowy ridges linking the various peaks of Monte Rosa lies an extraordinary landscape. Looking toward the French border on cloudless days,

visitors can recognize many peaks—especially the triangular Matterhorn. This photograph shows the Capanna Margherita shelter, the highest in Europe.

168-169 Parrotspitze, Punta Gnifetti, Zumsteinspitze, Dufourspitze, and Norden, all about 5,000 feet high, are the highest and most outstanding summits of the Monte Rosa group.

Seen from a plane as they emerge from the cascading ice and snow, the lofty peaks and glaciers of Europe's second highest mountain appear both majestic and forbidding.

170 *The soaring Brenta peaks divide four valleys in the heart of the Trentino region. Their awe-inspiring spires and cliffs offer an overview of the amazing panoramas and stark beauty typical of the Dolomites of Trentino and Veneto.*

171 *The Dolomites, as part of the eastern Alps are called, have craggy limestone peaks. They owe their fame to this particular type of rock, which allowed the gradual formation of spectacular, distinctively shaped mountain ranges, interrupted by deep, intensely green valleys.*

172-173 *The stunning Pale Group frames the hollow in which San Martino di Castrozza lies in the Val di Fiemme.*

174 *At dawn and just before dusk, the Dolomites appear to be ablaze, turning to amazing shades of red, pink, and purple. Often the mountain peaks remain bright with light from the setting sun even after the valleys are enveloped in darkness. Among the most spectacular peaks are the Cime di Lavaredo, the Brenta Dolomites, Sasso Lungo, and the Pale Group near San Martino. Cima Piccola, the lowest of the group, is actually the most difficult to climb by the traditional route.*

175 *Towering over the Val Gardena, Sassolungo is an awesome "cathedral" sculpted from limestone rock. Both Selva and the Siusi plateau afford breathtaking views of its distinctive peak.*

176-177 The Sella group is a popular destination for European climbers and hikers, with a high peak of almost 10,000 feet. It features sheer rock cliffs, gorges that are snow-covered even in summer, and amazingly evocative natural amphitheaters.

178-179 *For spectacular landscapes, look at the peaks of Tofane (at top) and Marmolada (at bottom). The latter, almost 11,000 feet high, features the only sizable glacier in the Dolomite chain. There are carved rocks (Gothic or pure fantasy), intriguing light effects, perpendicular mountain faces, and breathtaking panoramas. On the borders of Trentino, Alto Adige, and Veneto, these two peaks dominate the heart of the Dolomites.*

180-181 *Among the most important groups of the Adige region Alps, the Odle group offers hikers some of the most spectacular excursions. Still they are not well known.*

182-183 *The Gran Sasso is capped by the Corno Grande (over 9,000 feet), its bare rocky slopes stretching over an area of 21 miles. The scenery is majestic, with an abundance of ravines, craggy peaks, and boundless upland plains.*

184-185 *This photograph shows the crater of Vesuvius, the volcano that towers over Naples. It is famous for the eruption that destroyed the ancient cities of Pompeii and Herculaneum in 79 A.D.*

182 top *Monte Cimone is the highest peak in the Tuscan/Emilian Apennines at 7,000 feet, visible even from the distant plains of Lombardy. A military weather station has been installed on its slopes.*

182 center *The Abetone, astride Tuscany and Emilia, is clothed with a dense forest of larch, popular, beech, birch, and Adriatic oak. It is a popular resort for summer excursions and winter skiing.*

182 bottom *Abruzzo is a land of ancient crafts, peasants, and mighty mountains like the Maiella (shown) and the Gran Sasso d'Italia, glory of the region's landscape.*

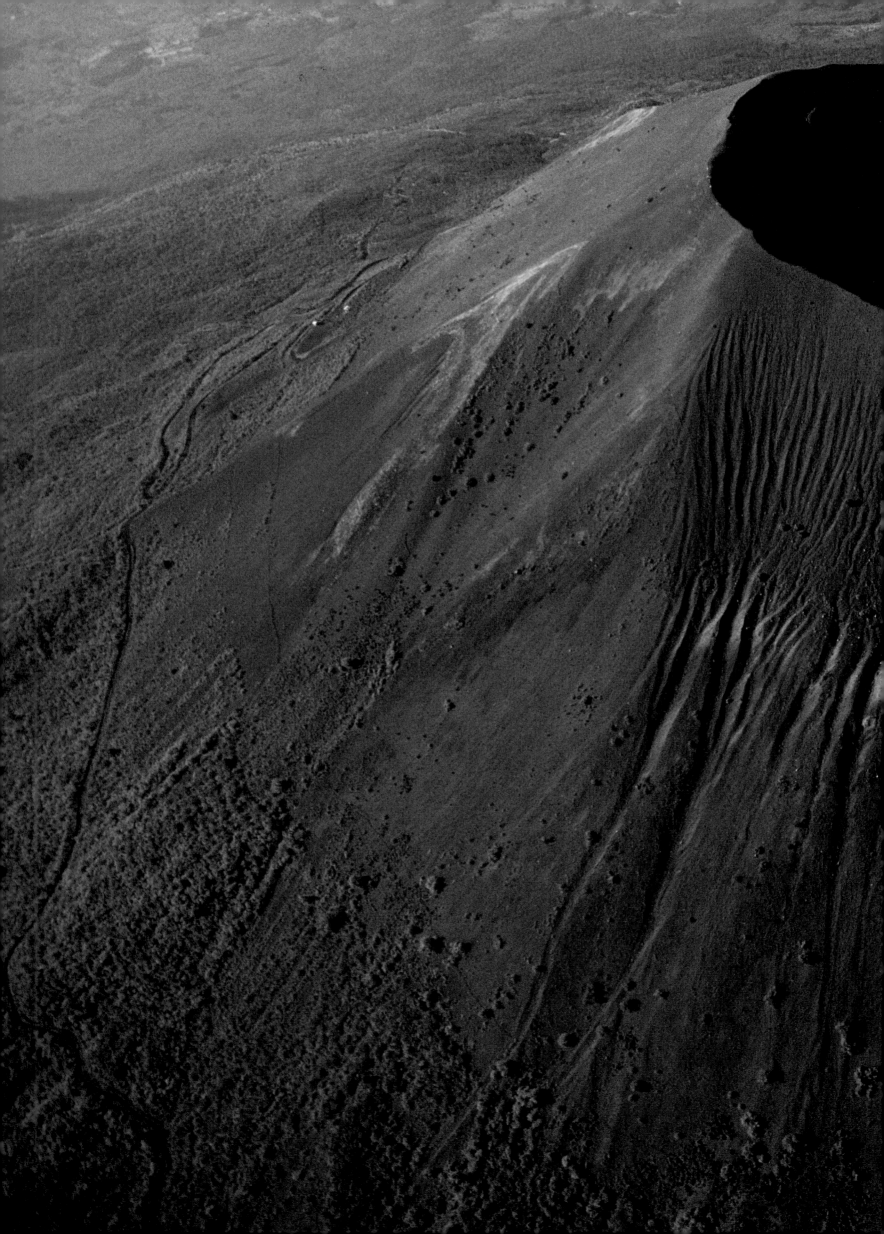

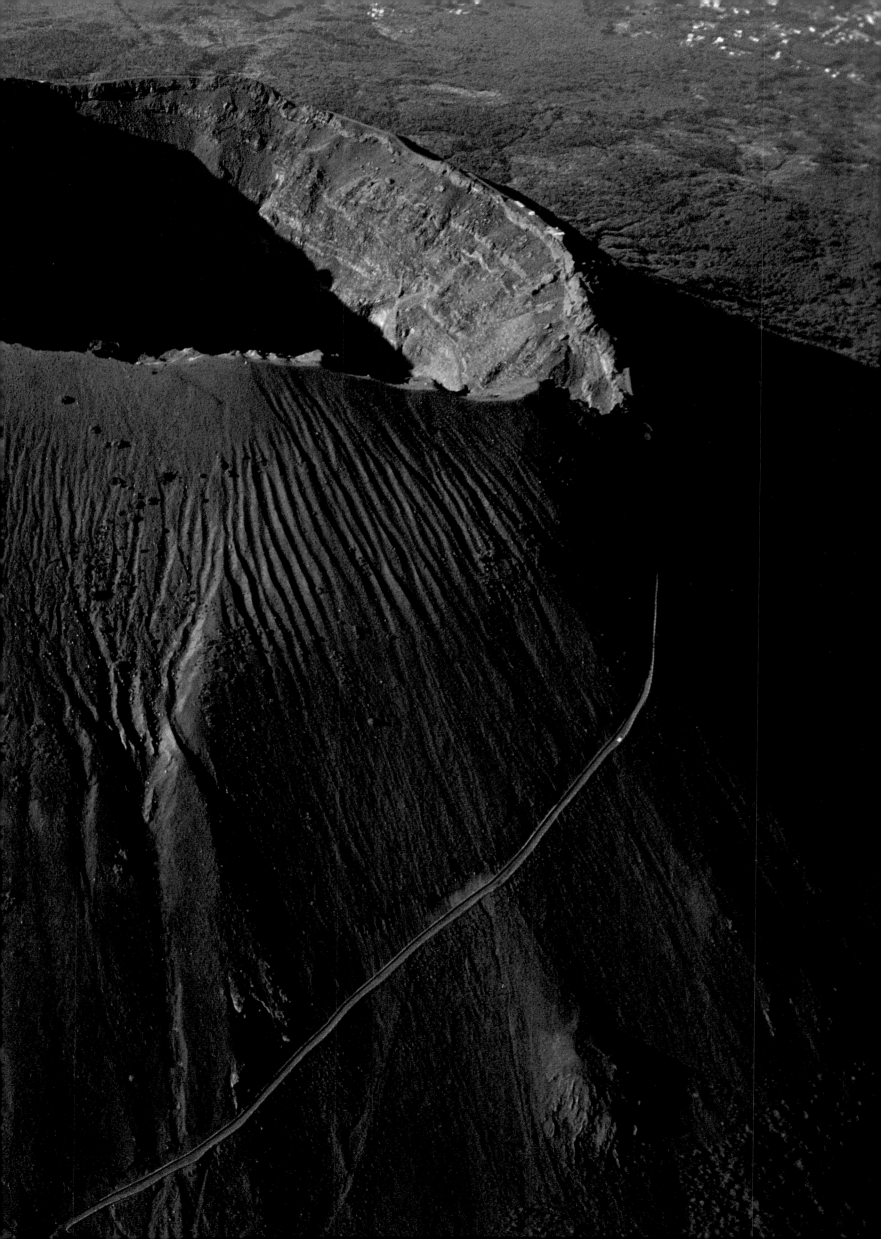

188-189 *This photograph shows unusual and mysterious scenery: a still-active volcano coated with snow. For many months of the year, Etna's 11,000-foot peak is covered with this white coat.*

ITALY'S DEEP BLUE SEA

190 *In ancient times, Portofino—the "port of dolphins" referred to by Pliny—was the home of coral fishermen. Today the village is frequented by international jet–setters; the traditional Ligurian houses overlooking the harbor have sky–high prices.*

191 *Traveling by boat past the famous verdant promontory of Portofino, you can reach the Abbazia di Fruttuoso di Capodimonte, built by the Doria family in the 13th century.*

193 *Monterosso is the most important of the Cinque Terre, one of the few with a sandy beach. Manarola is the most picturesque village, but its shores are without sand.*

192 left *The Cinque Terre (Monterosso al Mare, Vernazza, Corniglia, Manarola, and Riomaggiore) offer one of the most spectacular and dramatic landscapes in Liguria. The villages cling to the cliffs near age–old terraced vineyards that produce the fine Cinque Terre wine, among the best–known in Italy.*

192 top right *Also on the Riviera di Levante is another typical tiny village called Sori, which looks out onto a small bay nestling in the Golfo Paradiso.*

192 bottom right *Nervi, closer to Genoa, has many handsome 19th– and early 20th–century villages and houses.*

194 top Talamone, with its colorful harbor, is possibly the best known beach resort of the Maremma. In the last ten years, proximity to the fascinating Parco dell'Uccellina nature reserve has caused tourism to boom.

194 bottom Porto Santo Stefano was founded as a fishing village in the 15th century. It experienced its most prosperous period two centuries later, under Spanish rule.

194-195 The shores surrounding the rugged promontory of Monte Argentario offer glorious scenery in abundance; Porto Ercole is one of the area's most picturesque resorts.

195 top *Ansedonia owes its fame to the natural beauty of its coast and its rich history. The town was a Roman trading post in both republican and imperial eras. Its magnificent location made it a popular resort, as is evident from remains of a Roman villa discovered at Torre della Tagliata.*

196 bottom left *Giglio Porto is the island's busiest tourist center. Still visible are the remains of a Roman patrician villa, half hidden among vineyards.*

196 top right and 197 *The shores of Tuscany are immensely popular with Italian and foreign tourists alike. The island of Elba is a stunning mosaic of land- and seascapes; its main town and entrance door is Porto Ferraio.*

196 center right *The little islands around Elba include Pianosa, Giannultri, Gorgona, Montecristo, and the wild and splendid Isola del Giglio (shown here).*

196 bottom right *Dominating Campese, one of three villages on the island of Giglio, is a cylindrical castle tower erected at the time of Ferdinand I.*

198 top *The only low–lying island of the Tuscan archipelago is called Pianos; appropriately,* piano *means "flat" in Italian.*

198-199 *To the north of Capraia, on the island of Gorgona, the vegetation is only partly natural. A prison farm operates on the island, growing produce on artificially created terraces.*

199 top *Giannutri is the southernmost island of the whole Tuscan group. Much frequented by underwater divers, it boasts the remains of an impressive Roman villa, dating from the 1st century* A.D.

199 bottom *Montecristo is entirely owned by the Italian state. For many years a game preserve of the House of Savoy, this splendid nature reserve can be visited only with permission from the authorities.*

200-201 *Capraia, one-third of its land area farmed by inmates of an open prison, is one of the gems of the Tuscan archipelago. The sea bed beneath its translucent waters is exceptionally rich in marine life. Its hilly terrain, marked by deep folds known as* vadi, *is almost entirely covered by the Mediterranean brush, home to particularly interesting flora and fauna.*

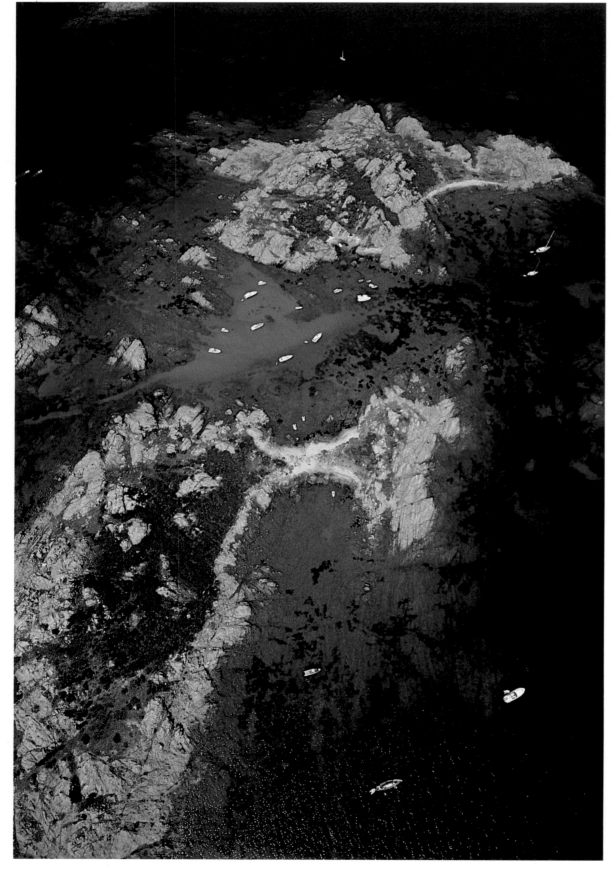

202 *The Costa Smeralda, in northern Sardinia, is a paradise of rocky bays and islets and crystal-clear waters, now dotted with many vacation resorts.*

203 *Not only does Caprera offer an idyllic natural setting, it is also famous as the place where Garibaldi spent his last days.*

204-205 *Facing the Costa Smeralda are the famously beautiful islands of La Maddalena, and the islet of Mortorio (shown here), a tropical oasis in the Mediterranean.*

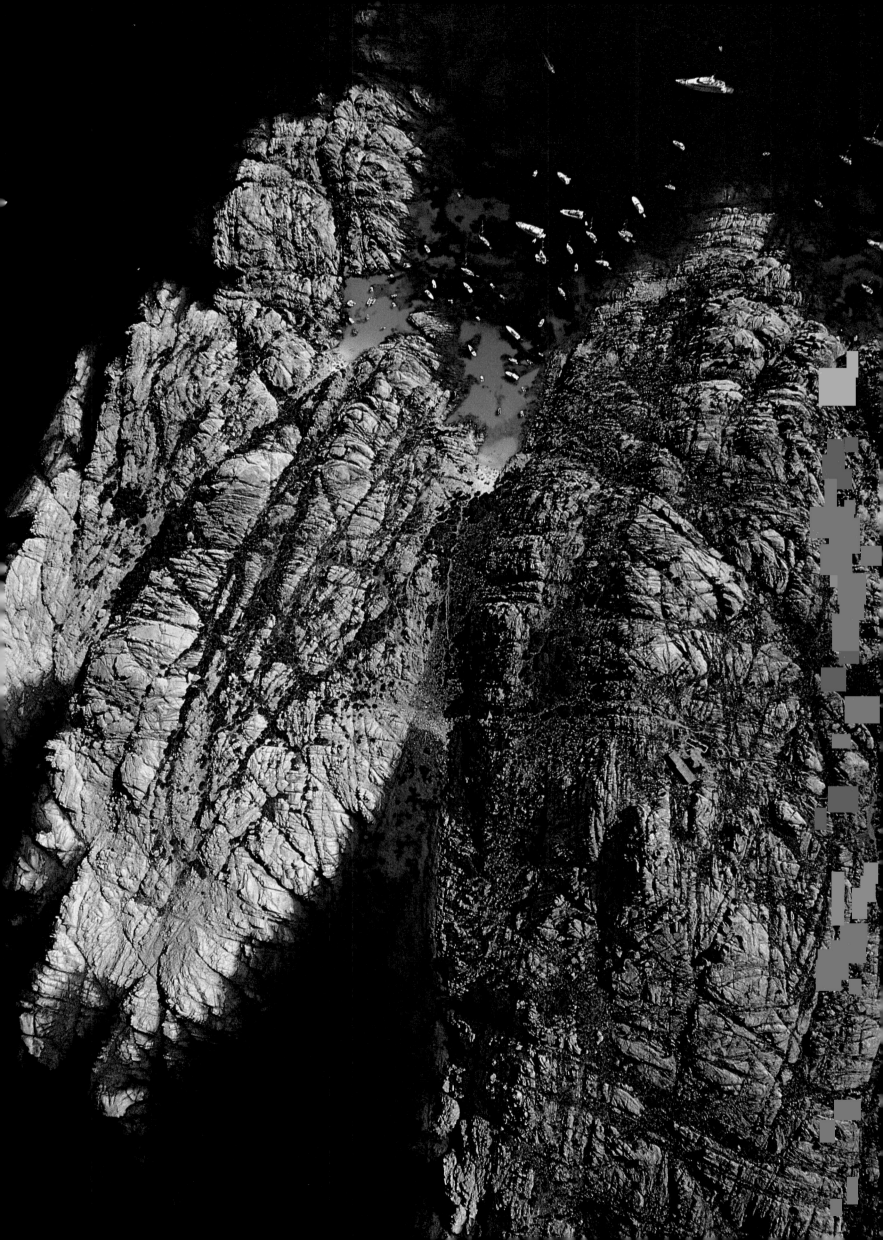

206-207 *Three hundred days a year of white sands, crystal–clear waters, and brilliant blue skies: all this and more is offered by the shores of Sardinia, where a deserted beach or cove can always be found.*

208-209 *Porto Cervo is the most celebrated tourist village and natural harbor of the Costa Smeralda. Villas are dotted here and there around its deep, fjord–like bay, at the foot of the gentle slopes that frame the resort.*

210 top *The island of San Pietro can be reached by ferry from the little town of Calasetta, on the island of Sant'Antico. Only one road crosses San Pietro, from Carloforte to Capo Sandalo.*

210 center *The pond of Is Benas is a great marsh populated by birds of every species. Thanks to a canal, Is Benas is connected at certain times of the year with Sale Porcus, the second of three ponds near Capo Mannu.*

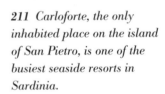

210 bottom *The promontory of Capo Mannu, in the province of Oristano, is dominated by a lighthouse and by a little old tower. The promontory is a succession of tall cliffs shaped by centuries of wind and water erosion. Thanks to the dense marine vegetation, the water looks dark green.*

211 *Carloforte, the only inhabited place on the island of San Pietro, is one of the busiest seaside resorts in Sardinia.*

212 *Cagliari, Sardinia's capital, is wedged between beaches, hills, and inland salt lagoons populated by huge numbers of birds, including flamingoes.*

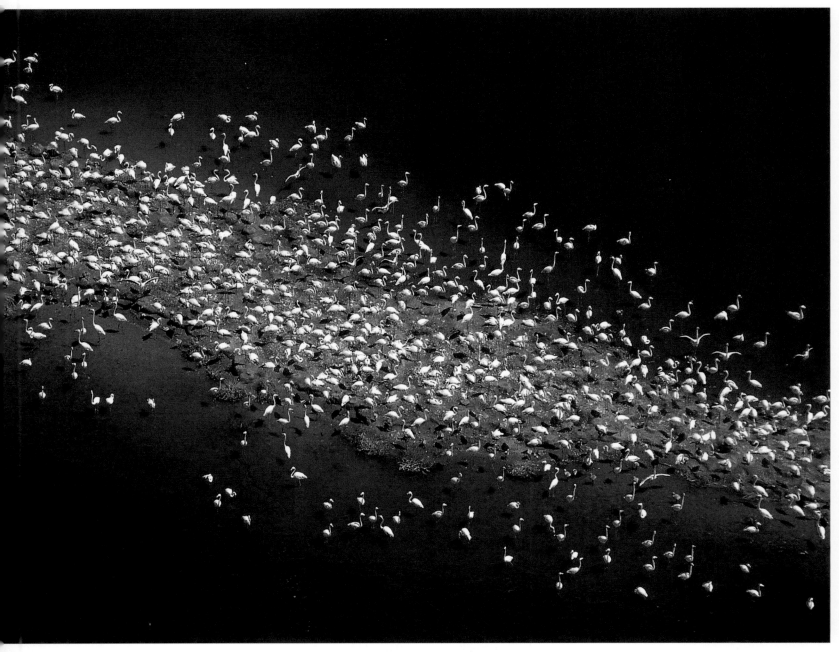

213 *For centuries, Cagliari has enjoyed a favorable location along Mediterranean trade routes. The economy of the city is based not only on trade but also on a modest industrial sector. The production of salt is of major importance.*

214 *The island of Ponza, five miles long, is the largest of the Pontino archipelago. Remains of Roman villas have been unearthed near Ponza, the main town.*

215 *Conquered by the Romans (who used the island as a parking place for undesirables), Ponza was long troubled by Saracen raids before it fell under Bourbon rule. Many testimonies to its Roman past are still evident, but now the scene is dominated by more recent Mediterranean–style buildings, with characteristic flat roofs. The island's great tourist appeal has led to intensive property development around the village of Ponza.*

216-217 and 216 bottom
Emerging between Ischia and Capo Miseno is the small island of Procida, once inhabited only by fishermen but now a bustling tourist center. The typical Mediterranean–style buildings accent the shores and interior of the island.

217 top *The Pontine islands off the shores of Lazio are of volcanic origin. Zannone, a microscopic island less than one square mile in size, is thick with vegetation. A third of the bird species that nest in Italy can be spotted on this island at various times of the year.*

217 center *A wonderful image of Ventotene, taken from high above, shows the beauty of the sea washing this archipelago.*

217 bottom *Santo Stefano is one of the islands which form the archipelago facing the Lazio shore.*

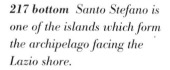

218 The castle on Ischia looks over the whole island, including the buildings below—an ancient cathedral, a monastery, and a 16th–century church. The only means of entering the castle is a bridge built by the Aragonese in the first half of the 15th century.

219 In the age-old town of Ischia fishing was long the mainstay of the economy. Tourism has now moved into the lead but fish and the sea have left a profound mark on the habits and customs of the local population.

220 bottom *Capri has been a popular resort for centuries, long frequented by visitors with aristocratic credentials. Part of its charm stems from the more illustrious tourists who have had homes here. As well as villas dating to the days of the Roman empire and handsome 19th-century residences, former fishermen's cottages converted by VIPs have helped enhance the island's reputation as an exclusive vacation haven.*

221 *The island of Capri would be unimaginable without its* faraglioni: *in slightly less than half a million years, the erosive action of the sea turned a promontory into three rocky crags.*

220-221 *Capri is a place of scenic splendors. Like Ischia, it is one of the best known islands of the Campania region and a favorite haunt of international jet-setters. Blessed by its geographical position, it offers a temperate climate for nine months of the year, unspoiled corners of natural beauty, and the irresistible delights of tiny squares and shady pergolas dotted about its main town.*

222 top In Positano, Amalfi, and Ravello—delightful resorts found along the panoramic coastal route— natural beauty and culture are inextricably mingled. Particularly lovely is Positano, with its little houses sloping down toward the sea on terraces separated only by winding stepped alleys.

222 bottom Cetrara is a picturesque fishing village overlooking the bay of Naples, not far from Sorrento. Dominated by Monte Falerzio, it has existed unchanged for many centuries.

222-223 *Sorrento and the Costiera Amalfitana are among southern Italy's most stunning gems. Separating the bays of Naples and Salerno is the Sorrentine peninsula, with its tip directly facing Capri. Many towns and villages lie on or close to its shores. The largest is Sorrento, a well–developed resort extending along a cliff at a dizzying height above the blue waters of the bay.*

224-225 Capo Vaticano, in Calabria, is only a few miles from Tropea, a picturesque town in the province of Vibo Valentia. The rocky promontory offers superb views, well–groomed beaches, and splendid sites for underwater diving.

226-227 The coasts of Calabria have translucent water, uncrowded bays, and an underwater world exceptionally rich in flora and fauna. It is an ideal setting for scuba diving and snorkeling.

228-229 *The town of Bagheria is well known among Sicily's many magnificent beach resorts. Palermo aristocrats built handsome villas here in the 17th and 18th centuries.*

228 top *The sea is the crowning glory of many Sicilian beauty spots. Shown here is Aci Trezza, a famous fishing center and tourist resort, only a few miles from Mount Etna.*

229 top *Taormina is framed by rocks and ocean, the glowering mass of Mount Etna and the lush vegetation of almond, olive, and orange groves. Apart from its stunning Roman theater and other ancient ruins, its atmosphere is thoroughly medieval, with crenellated buildings like the Palazzo Corvaia.*

229 bottom *The elegant beach resort of Mondello overlooks shores only a few miles from downtown Palermo, along the bay north of the city.*

230-231 *The Aeolian archipelago has seven main islands: the three largest neighboring ones (Vulcano, Lipari and Salina), plus Filicudi and Alicudi to the west, and Panarea and Stromboli to the north. Among the features of Stromboli (shown in these photos) are rocky shores and a still active volcano, rising to a height of 2,500 feet.*

232-233 *The vistas and vegetation of the Aeolian islands are world–famous. With its rugged cliffs and almost barren landscape, Alicudi (shown here) offers one of the wildest landscapes in the entire Mediterranean.*

232 bottom *The island of Vulcano is made up of three volcanoes, although only one is considered still active. It last erupted in 1890.*

233 top Panarea is the smallest island of the Aeolian group. Countless forms of marine life are to be seen in the clear waters off its shores, attracting many underwater divers.

233 center Filicudi has the remains of a prehistoric village. Numerous archaeological finds have been made on the Aeolion archipelago, including obsidian (volcanic "black glass") carved on Lipari in the Neolithic age and widely exported.

233 bottom Salina is the second largest island of the Aeolian archipelago, after Lipari. Its present name comes from the salt deposits in its southeast corner.

234 top *The largest of Sicily's smaller islands is Pantelleria. Of volcanic origin, its highest point is the crater of Montagna Grande.*

234 center *Favignana is the biggest of the Egadi Islands, the archipelago not far off the coast of Trapani. Like the other Sicilian islands, it was inhabited in prehistoric times.*

234 bottom *Levanzo is one of the Egadi Islands; it is well known for a cave called the Grotto del Genovese, where paintings and graffiti from the Paleolithic age have been discovered. Like Favignana, another island of this group, it has an important tuna–fishing fleet.*

234-235 *Sun, sea, and Mediterranean plants: together these add up to the stunning picture presented by Linosa, a tiny volcanic island slightly less than two square miles. Linosa, Lampedusa, and Lampione together form the Pelagic group.*

236-237 *The Tremiti islands, covered with rocks, vineyards, and pines, are situated off the northern shores of the Gargano peninsula in Puglia. There are four main islands. San Domino (in the background), the largest, is the only one with much vegetation, in particular a pine forest that runs down to the sea.*

236 top *Still partly protected by Angevin walls, the old town of Mola di Bari offers numerous vestiges of the ancient harbor area. The harbor was of great strategic importance at the time of the Crusades.*

237 top *In Puglia, the celebrated Gargano peninsula extends far into the Adriatic. High cliffs tower in the east.*

237 bottom *Among the most typical towns of Paglia are Santa Maria di Leuca, Mola, and Vieste, which occupies a rocky headland at the easternmost tip of the Gargano. The promontory where Santa Maria di Leuca is located lies beyond Otranto, at the very end of Italy's "heel." Along its rocky and often inaccessible shores are fascinating grottoes.*

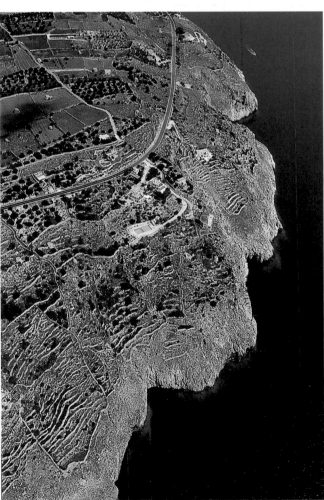

238-239 *The most striking features of Gallipoli are its houses, contrasting with the deep blue of the Ionian Sea, and its rocky shores. The town, shaped like an hourglass, is accented by the ancient fortress and the 17th–century bridge.*

240 The Castle of Fenis
was erected in the 14th
century by the powerful
Challant family, feudal
lords of the Valle d'Aosta.
Since then its awesome
mass, featuring a
pentagonal floor plan
and huge towers, have
dominated the valley
of the Dora Baltea.

AIR CONCESSIONS

Concession S.M.A No. 01-161 of 17.04.1997
Concession S.M.A No. 01-457 of 16.10.1996
Concession S.M.A No. 01-480 of 28.10.1996
Concession S.M.A No. 01-26 of 14.01.1997
Concession S.M.A No. 01-339 of 03.09.1996
Concession S.M.A No. 01-01 of 02.01.1997
Concession S.M.A No. 01-338 of 03.09.1996
Concession S.M.A No. 01-337 of 03.09.1996
Concession S.M.A No. 01-297 of 07.08.1996
Concession S.M.A No. 01-336 of 03.09.1996